John J. Segreto

# CHEESECAKE MADNESS

**Biscuit Books, Inc.**
**Newton, Massachusetts**

Cover design by Charles Kreloff
Illustration by Bob Hiemstra

Biscuit Books, Inc.
P. O. Box 610159
Newton, Massachusetts 02161


ISBN 0-9643600-2-0 (previously 0-671-50474-6, paper)

Printed and bound in the United States of America

00 99 98 97 96                    5 4 3 2 1

Library of Congress Cataloging-in-Publication Data
Segreto, John J.
      Cheesecake madness / John J. Segreto. — 1st Biscuit Books ed.
         p.    cm.
      Reprint. Originally published: New York: Macmillan, 1981.
      Includes index.
      ISBN 0-9643600-2-0 (cloth)
      1. Cheesecake (Cookery)      I. Title.
TX773.S356  1996
641.8′653—dc20                                              96-42904
                                                                CIP

I dedicate this book to WINNIE,
my ever-loving wife and friend.

# Contents

## Cheesecakes with Nuts   78

## Cheesecakes from Around the World   101

# REFRIGERATOR CHEESECAKES

## Simple Cheesecakes  147

# Acknowledgments

Special thanks are due to the many people who encouraged and supported me in the writing of this book. First among these is my dear wife, Winnie, who sustained me in spirit and also acted as my chief reviewer.

Next, the dear friends who unhesitatingly lent assistance in research, in sharing recipes and techniques, and in testing and tasting the recipes and cheesecakes.

Finally, my particular thanks to Macmillan's senior editors Frank Wilkinson and Toni Lopopolo, their assistant Linda Benvin, and the editorial and production staff, all of whom labored with such enthusiasm in producing this cookbook.

# CHEESECAKE
# MADNESS

# Introduction

From early times, people have experimented with cheese cookery. Cheesecake baking has remained a favorite kitchen art and eating pleasure for some 2,800 years.

Between 800 to 700 B.C. the first-known cheesecake was created in ancient Greece, on the island of Samos in the Aegean Sea. Small cheesecakes were fed to athletes for energy during the first Olympic Games on the Isle of Delos in 776 B.C. and also to children as a reward for good behavior and excellence in their studies and sports.

Thereafter cheesecakes gained tremendous social popularity in ancient Greece, becoming the wedding cakes for the rich. In the Greek city of Argos it was customary for young brides to bake and serve little cheesecakes to friends of the groom, which resulted in the wedding-cake tradition.

The basic recipe and ingredients for the first cheesecake were recorded by Athenaeus, a Greek writer, in about A.D. 230: "Take cheese and pound it till smooth and pasty; put cheese in a brazen sieve; add honey and spring wheat flour. Heat in one mass, cool, and serve."

The Greeks were not the only ancient peoples to practice cheese cookery; so did the ancient Romans, who built special kitchens primarily for the purpose of making cheese and cooking it. The ancient Romans considered cheese a food not only for the rich but for everyone. Average Roman citizens made or purchased little cheesecakes for their own eating pleasure or to reward their children with tasty snacks or delicacies, as we give candies, cookies, and cakes to children today.

The Roman Empire spread throughout Europe as the Roman army under Julius Caesar overran and conquered the Continent. Traveling northward through their newly conquered lands, the Romans discovered that the food customs and habits of others involved cheese to a great extent. Caesar was fascinated with the Germanic diet's dependence on cheese cookery, and when the Romans conquered Britain, they found that the Britons also had a primitive cheese—the earliest Cheshire. They discovered that throughout the Continent milk and cheese were customary dietary staples.

Travelers, merchants, and Crusaders returned with recipes and a knowledge of the techniques of cheesemaking from their trips into the East and the Mediterranean area, thus spreading the art of cheese cookery throughout Europe. By A.D. 1000 dairying, cheesemaking, and cheese cookery were firmly established in the Scandinavian countries, England, and the countries of northwestern Europe.

In Europe, the Church and monks began to develop the art of cheese cookery by producing various cheese dishes and cheesecakes for nourishment and income. During the eleventh century, Roquefort cheese was used by the monks as the basic ingredient for making cheesecakes. These European cheese adventurers taught the art of cheesemaking and cheese cookery to those who later migrated to the Americas, who in turn brought with them the important knowledge and experience of fine cheesecake baking and quality cheese cuisine.

Not until 1872 did cheesecake baking, as we know it today, become practical and popular. This was due to William Lawrence, who developed the method of producing cream cheese in Chester, New York. At about the same time a dairyman living in South Edmeston, New York, developed a fine cream cheese for the Empire Cheese Company, later to be known by the name Philadelphia Brand Cream Cheese.

Since the early 1900s, cheesecakes have been a recognized popular dessert in the finest restaurants and a mark of excellence of the most famous chefs in New York, Chicago, San Francisco, New Orleans, Paris, Rome, and London.

The advent of the American supermarket in the 1940s brought with it a great consumer demand for more and more dairy products. The dairy industry has continued to grow to meet ever-growing demands. Today in each supermarket can be found a variety of cream cheeses, processed and natural cheeses, sour creams, light and heavy creams, and a variety of low-fat and low-calorie dairy products. Canned fruits, nuts, extracts, sugars, eggs, and juices—all important ingredients in making cheesecakes—are easily found in supermarkets and local grocery stores.

Of all the foods in which cream cheese is the main ingredient, the most favored is cheesecake. The popularity of the cheesecake has continued to grow. Throughout the country, people have established cheesecake clubs and baking and recipe contests; food magazines featuring many interesting and unusual recipes tantalize our taste buds and appetites.

Many bakeries, restaurants, and other food purveyors pride themselves on making and serving the "best cheesecake." Who can know which cheesecake is the "best" when there are so many different ones, each with its own particular flavor?

The definition of a custard is a mixture of eggs, milk, sugar, and flavoring produced by either boiling, baking, or refrigerating. Since the ingredients of cheesecakes are primarily eggs, milk, milk products, sugar, and flavoring and the mixtures are either baked or refrigerated, it must be noted that a cheesecake is primarily a custard. By changing the ratios and amounts of cheese, milk, eggs, sugar, and flavorings and balancing them with baking times and temperatures, we can create a great variety of delicious and unusual cheesecakes.

The popular quiche, a custard pie, is similar to cheesecake, with the exception that many times ingredients are chosen that replace sugar with meats, vegetables, and spices. Again, by changing the ratios and amounts of the ingredients and the cooking times, a great variety of quiches have been created.

Cheesecake making is fun; it's a challenge, a game, an adventure, and an art. By picking and choosing different relative proportions and quantities of ingredients and by balancing times and temperatures, we, too, can make the "best cheesecake." The adventurous can emerge connoisseurs of cheesecake.

Since there are an infinite variety of cheesecakes to suit as many tastes, this book selects 101 unusual and choice cheesecake recipes, as well as providing added information collected from a number of good cooks, chefs, and fine restaurants—all designed for your best cheesecake making and eating enjoyment.

## How to Make a Low-Calorie Cheesecake

It is very easy to create a low-calorie cheesecake. You simply replace the ingredients that have the higher caloric values with similar ones having fewer calories.

### HOW TO CALCULATE CALORIES

Most prepared ingredients found in the supermarket contain their caloric values on the package label for immediate reference. However, here is an example of how to calculate the number of calories in both a given recipe and an individual serving, using the caloric value chart and measurement charts contained in the following pages. The example used is Traditional Cheesecake, the complete recipe for which can be found on page 17.

| CRUST | 1 cup graham cracker crumbs | 336 |
|---|---|---|
| | 2 tablespoons sweet butter | 200 |
| | 1 tablespoon granulated sugar | 45 |
| FILLING | 1½ pounds cream cheese | 2,640 |
| | 1¼ cups granulated sugar | 900 |
| | 1½ teaspoons vanilla extract | 9 |
| | 4 eggs | 280 |
| | 1 cup sour cream | 480 |
| | 1 cup heavy cream | 480 |
| | 1½ teaspoons powdered sugar | 20 |
| | TOTAL NUMBER OF CALORIES | 5,890 |

5,890 calories divided by 8 slices or servings = 672 calories per serving; divided by 16 slices or servings = 336 calories per serving.

Here is an example of how to create a low-calorie Traditional Cheesecake by substitution of ingredients:

| CRUST | 1 cup vanilla wafer crumbs | 276 |
|---|---|---|
| | 2 tablespoons sweet butter | 200 |
| | 1 tablespoon sugar substitute | 20 |
| FILLING | 1½ pounds imitation cream cheese | 1,200 |
| | ½ cup sugar substitute | 160 |
| | 1½ teaspoons vanilla extract | 9 |
| | 4 eggs | 280 |
| | 1 cup sour cream | 480 |
| | 1 cup non-dairy creamer (e.g., Perx, etc.) | 125 |
| | TOTAL NUMBER OF CALORIES | 3,250 |

3,250 calories divided by 8 slices or servings = 406 calories per serving; divided by 16 slices or servings = 203 calories per serving.

# Caloric Values
## of Most Ingredients
### Used in Cheesecakes

| FOOD CATEGORY | INGREDIENT | MEASURE | CALORIES |
|---|---|---|---|
| CHEESES | Cream cheese | 8 ounces | 880 |
| | Imitation cream cheese | 8 ounces | 400 |
| | Creamed cottage cheese | 8 ounces | 217 |
| | Low-fat cottage cheese | 8 ounces | 164 |
| | Dry-curd cottage cheese | 8 ounces | 123 |
| | Ricotta (whole milk) | 8 ounces | 380 |
| | Ricotta (skim milk) | 8 ounces | 340 |
| | Pot cheese | 8 ounces | 200 |
| | Farmer cheese | 8 ounces | 223 |
| CREAMS | Sour cream | ½ cup | 240 |
| | Heavy cream | ½ cup | 240 |
| | Imitation heavy cream | ½ cup | 125 |
| | Light cream or half-and-half | ½ cup | 240 |
| | Yogurt (plain) | 1 cup | 125 |
| BUTTER | Butter | 1 tablespoon | 100 |
| | Margarine | 1 tablespoon | 100 |
| EGGS | Egg | 1 medium | 70 |
| SWEETENERS | Granulated sugar | 1 tablespoon | 45 |
| | Granulated sugar | 1 cup | 720 |
| | Corn syrup | 1 cup | 928 |
| | Honey | 1 cup | 1280 |
| | Maple syrup | 1 cup | 1040 |
| | Imitation sugar (saccharine) | 1 cup | 320 |
| | Imitation sugar (saccharine) | 1 tablespoon | 20 |
| CRACKERS | Graham cracker crumbs | 1 cup | 336 |
| | Vanilla wafer crumbs | 1 cup | 276 |
| | Chocolate wafer crumbs | 1 cup | 588 |
| | Zwieback crumbs | 1 cup | 582 |

| FOOD CATEGORY | INGREDIENT | MEASURE | CALORIES |
|---|---|---|---|
| CRACKERS (Cont.) | Gingersnap crumbs | 1 cup | 252 |
| | Butter cookie crumbs | 1 cup | 324 |
| | Social Tea crumbs | 1 cup | 456 |
| FLAVORINGS | Cocoa (unsweetened) | 1 tablespoon | 21 |
| | Baking chocolate | 1 ounce | 145 |
| | Extracts | 1 teaspoon | 6 |
| | Jams and preserves | 1 tablespoon | 55 |
| | Liquor and liqueurs | 1 ounce | 70 |
| NUTS | Almonds | 1 cup | 850 |
| | Cashews | 1 cup | 785 |
| | Coconut (shredded) | 1 cup | 344 |
| | Pecans | 1 cup | 740 |
| | Walnuts | 1 cup | 650 |
| | Hazelnuts | 1 cup | 775 |
| FRUITS | Apricots (canned in syrup) | 1 cup | 220 |
| | Banana | 1 medium | 100 |
| | Blackberries | 1 cup | 85 |
| | Blueberries | 1 cup | 90 |
| | Cherries (canned in syrup) | 1 cup | 105 |
| | Mandarin oranges (canned in syrup) | 1 cup | 125 |
| | Pineapple (canned in syrup) | 1 cup | 190 |
| | Raisins | 1 ounce | 80 |
| | Strawberries | 1 cup | 55 |
| | Lemon juice | 1 tablespoon | 4 |
| FLOURS | All-purpose white flour | 1 cup | 364 |
| | Whole wheat flour | 1 cup | 410 |
| | Cornstarch | 1 tablespoon | 29 |
| GELATIN | Gelatin (unflavored) | 1 ounce | 30 |

# General Cheesecake Information and Helpful Hints

BAKING

Prepare the springform pan by first buttering the bottom and sides and then lining the bottom with a sheet of baking paper cut to size. This enables you to remove the cheesecake from the bottom of the pan more easily.

Another possible method is to cut to size a sturdy piece of cardboard and wrap it neatly in aluminum foil. After placing this disk into the springform pan, butter the disk and sides of the pan. This method is ideal if making a cheesecake to give away, for you need not use the bottom of the pan to transport the cake.

Next, press or pat the crumb mixture with a spoon onto the bottom and or sides of the springform pan to create a smoothly packed crust. Refrigerate or chill the pan in the freezer for 15 to 30 minutes or until the crust becomes fairly firm so that, when the prepared cheesecake mixture is poured on top of it, the crumb mixture will not flake apart or crumble and blend into the filling.

Cheesecakes often crack while baking; some rise, and some later fall. But this does not affect the taste and appearance of the cheesecake. Keep in mind that cheesecakes, like custards, do not take kindly to sudden changes in temperature, so *do not open the oven door during baking*.

To keep the final cheesecake moist and creamy, remember that the general baking method stated in recipes is to place the springform pan into a larger pan that contains enough water to rise one inch up the sides of the springform pan. This method is commonly known as the bain-marie method.

Once the cheesecake has thoroughly cooled and set, carefully remove the bottom and sides of the springform pan.

For best results most cheesecakes should be refrigerated over night, then removed from the refrigerator at least 2 hours before serving.

REFRIGERATION

Cheesecakes are usually kept under refrigeration to retain their freshness and moisture. However, most cheesecakes can be kept in the freezer for a week or two and later thawed before serving. To freeze a cheesecake, prepare it as if it were to be served promptly, then freeze the cake as is for at least 6 hours. Next, remove the cake from the freezer and wrap it in freezer-weight foil (.0015 gauge). For long freezing, double-wrap the cheesecake with freezer paper over the freezer foil. At room temperature thaw the frozen cheesecake in its wrapping at least 2 to 3 hours before unwrapping. Then place the cake on a serving dish and let it thaw completely at room temperature.

READING A RECIPE

Read the recipe thoroughly before going shopping. It is important that you completely understand the recipe and process described. Before you begin work on the recipe, clear off your work surface and place all of the ingredients before you. Start with the ingredients that are kept in the refrigerator: Think ahead, especially, regarding ingredients that need to be softened before being worked with, such as cream cheese and butter. Carefully select the bowls, pan, utensils, and measuring cups and spoons and place them at your ready reach. Now you are fully prepared to begin cooking.

MEASURING

Measuring cups, usually made of glass or plastic, have a ¼-inch gap between the top measure and the pouring lip. Be sure that the cup is at all times at eye level when you fill it, otherwise you can be off the measurement by quite a bit.

Measuring spoons are carefully calibrated and should not be confused with ordinary everyday spoons. The standard tablespoon holds ⅟₃₂ of a pint. Four tablespoons equal ¼ cup, 3 teaspoons equal 1 tablespoon; and a dessertspoon holds 2 teaspoons. When a recipe calls for a teaspoon or a tablespoon, it means a level spoonful, that is, even with the rim of the bowl of the spoon.

WEIGHTS AND MEASURES

For liquid and dry measurements use the standard measuring spoons and cups. All measurements should be level.

| | |
|---|---|
| A dash | less than ⅛ teaspoon |
| 3 teaspoons | 1 tablespoon |
| 2 tablespoons | ⅛ cup |
| 4 tablespoons | ¼ cup |
| 5⅓ tablespoons | ⅓ cup |
| 8 tablespoons | ½ cup |
| 10⅔ tablespoons | ⅔ cup |
| 12 tablespoons | ¾ cup |
| 16 tablespoons | 1 cup |
| ½ pint | 1 cup |
| 1 pint | 2 cups |
| 8 ounces | 1 cup |
| 1 ounce of liquid | 2 tablespoons |
| 8 ounces | ½ pound |
| 16 ounces | 1 full pound |

# Specialty
## Measurements

| INGREDIENT | QUANTITY | EQUIVALENT MEASURE |
|---|---|---|
| Almonds | 1 pound | 2½ cups |
| Apples | 1 pound | 5 cups |
| Apricots | 1 pound | 3 cups |
| Bananas | 1 pound | 2½ cups |
| Butter | 1 pound | 2 cups |
| Cream cheese | 3 ounces | 6 tablespoons |
| Chocolate, unsweetened | 1 square | 1 ounce |
| Cocoa | 1 pound | 4 cups |
| Cream, heavy | ½ pint | 1 cup (2 cups whipped) |
| Coconut | 1 pound, shredded | 6 cups |
| Crackers and wafers | about 40 crackers | 1 pound |
| Eggs | 4 to 6, whole | 1 cup |
| Flour | 1 pound | 4 to 4½ cups |
| Graham crackers | 15 crushed | 1 cup |
| Lemon juice | 1 medium lemon | 3 tablespoons juice |
| Lemon rind | 1 medium lemon | 2 tablespoons grated rind |
| Milk, evaporated | 14½-ounce can | 1⅔ cup |
| Milk, sweetened, condensed | 14-ounce can | 1⅓ cup |
| Nuts | 1 pound, shelled | about 4 cups |
| Orange juice | 1 medium orange | ½ cup juice |
| Orange rind | 1 medium orange | 2½ tablespoons grated rind |
| Sugar, granulated | ½ pound | 1 cup* |
| Vanilla extract and other liquid flavorings | 1 ounce | 2 tablespoons |

* Sift the granulated sugar before measuring if there are lumps.

SUBSTITUTIONS

CHOCOLATE    3 tablespoons powdered cocoa plus 1 tablespoon
             butter.

SUGAR        ¾ cup honey for each 1 cup sugar and reduce liquid
             in the recipe by ¼ cup for each 1 cup of honey
             used.

BUTTER       Whenever possible use sweet butter rather than
             salted butter; salted butter has a greater tendency
             to burn than does sweet butter.

CRUSTS

Preparing a graham cracker, wafer, or biscuit crust is very
simple. Place a number of crackers on a sheet of wax paper, and
with a rolling pin or large jar, roll the crackers until they are
crushed into fine crumbs. In a bowl combine the cracker crumbs
with sugar and butter or margarine and blend the mixture with
your fingers, a fork, or a pastry blender. Make sure that the
crumb mixture is completely worked in with the butter or margarine. Then, with a spoon or your fingers, press or pat the mixture onto the bottom and/or sides of a well-buttered springform
pan.

FILLINGS

Cheesecake fillings comprise cheese, sugar, eggs, milk products,
and flavorings. A variety of cheeses and flavorings are used.
Cheeses such as cream cheese, ricotta cheese, cottage cheese, pot
cheese, farmer cheese, and others are used as the base for cheesecakes. The flavorings vary as much as the kinds of cheeses that
are used. Flavorings such as vanilla, almond, and various other
extracts; lemon and orange juices and rinds; fruits; nuts; and
liqueurs are used with ease and enjoyable results.

TOPPINGS

Toppings can be either very simple or very creative. They can vary from the simple sprinkling of powdered sugar to a creative decoration for a birthday or anniversary. With the use of a sour cream base with fruits or nuts, a commercially prepared fruit topping, or whipped cream, a most attractive cake can be created. There are no basic rules to follow where toppings are concerned.

SPRINGFORM PANS

The springform pan is the most popular and most useful pan to use when making a cheesecake. It is a loose-bottomed pan that molds the cheesecake and comes in various sizes—5-inch, 7-inch, 8½-inch, 9-inch, and so on; the most popular springform size is the 9-inch. A nonstick finish or a highly polished finish makes it easier to get the cake out after baking, but care must be taken not to mar the finish and shape of the pan. Never use a knife to pry or force the cake out of the pan. If the springform pan is kept clean and carefully stored, it should last a long time. It should be cleaned immediately after the cheesecake has been taken out of it, especially the outer ring. When the outer ring is released, it usually retains some of the sides of the cake on it. Therefore, clean it very well and be careful not to damage the spring lock.

## Using Blenders, Mixers, and Food Processors

There are many electric appliances that contribute greatly to the ease of preparing cheesecakes. Using blenders, mixers, and modern food processors to prepare cheesecakes can be fun and timesaving. These useful appliances make the mixing process more thorough and take most of the labor out of making cheesecakes.

Blenders are mostly used for liquefying, chopping, grinding, and pureeing. They can be both a time-saver and a cost-saver. Using the blender to puree fresh fruits or to chop nuts and then to blend and combine various fruits and flavors together to form new and interesting flavors and results can be very exciting and rewarding.

Electric mixers are invaluable for creaming butter, beating cream and cream cheese, and beating eggs, batters, and mixtures. Some mixers are equipped with only one set of blades, which are used for everything, whereas others come with several blades and attachments for various uses. Bladed beaters and mixers are used for creaming and beating, wire ones for whisking and whipping, and spiral hooks for combining mixtures such as pastry dough or cracker crumbs.

The modern and popular food processor combines many of the functions of electric mixers and blenders. Today's food processor kneads, mixes, whips, creams, grinds, purees, slices, and shreds. What really sets the food processor apart from mixers and blenders, though, is its ability to do so many things more efficiently, rapidly, accurately, and easily. Using a food processor to prepare batters and mixtures for cheesecakes will save you time, money, and labor.

# BAKED
# CHEESECAKES

# Plain Cheesecakes

## TRADITIONAL CHEESECAKE

*This is one of the easiest cheesecakes to make and the result is very satisfying—not too sweet and extremely light and moist. A rare treat for the beginner and a most enjoyable introduction to cheesecake-making.*

CRUST
: 1 cup graham cracker crumbs
  1 tablespoon granulated sugar

  2 tablespoons sweet butter, softened

FILLING
: 1½ pounds cream cheese, softened
  1¼ cups of granulated sugar
  1½ teaspoons vanilla extract

  4 eggs
  1 cup sour cream
  1 cup heavy cream
  1½ teaspoons powdered sugar

PAN
: 10-inch springform pan

CRUST  In a small mixing bowl, combine the graham cracker crumbs, sugar, and butter. Blend well with fingers, fork, or pastry blender. Press or pat the mixture onto the bottom of a well-buttered springform pan. Chill in the freezer or refrigerator for about 15 minutes.

**FILLING**  In a large bowl, beat the cream cheese, sugar, vanilla, and 1 egg until very smooth. Add the remaining 3 eggs, the sour cream, and the heavy cream and beat until smooth. Pour the mixture into the chilled springform pan and bake in a preheated 350°F oven for 1¼ hours. When done, turn off the oven and allow the cake to cool in the open oven for 1 hour. Then remove the cake from the oven and place it on a wire rack until completely cooled. Refrigerate for about 2 hours. Remove the sides of the springform pan and sprinkle the top of the cake with the powdered sugar before serving.

---

# STANDARD PLAIN
# CHEESECAKE

*A cheesecake that truly melts in the mouth—very light and creamy, proven to be a favorite with cheesecake lovers. Sprinkling the top with chopped walnuts or pecans and placing a cherry in the center gives this cake an ice-cream-sundae look.*

| | | |
|---|---|---|
| **CRUST** | 1¼ cups graham cracker crumbs<br>¼ cup granulated sugar | 1 teaspoon vanilla extract<br>4 tablespoons (½ stick) sweet butter, softened |
| **FILLING** | 1½ pounds cream cheese, softened<br>1 cup granulated sugar | 5 eggs<br>1 teaspoon vanilla extract |
| **TOPPING** | 1½ cups sour cream<br>1 tablespoon granulated sugar | 1 teaspoon vanilla extract<br>1 cup chopped or ground walnuts |
| **PAN** | 9-inch springform pan | |

CRUST In a small mixing bowl, combine the graham cracker crumbs, sugar, vanilla, and butter. Blend well with fingers, fork, or pastry blender. Press or pat the mixture onto the bottom of a well-buttered springform pan. Chill in the freezer or refrigerator for about 30 minutes.

FILLING In a large bowl, beat the cream cheese, sugar, and 1 egg until very smooth, then add the remaining 4 eggs, one at a time, making sure that the mixture is smooth after beating in each addition. Add the vanilla and continue to beat until very smooth and creamy. Pour the mixture into the chilled pan and bake in a preheated 375°F oven for 45 minutes, then turn off the oven and allow the cake to sit in the closed oven for 2 hours. Transfer the cake to a wire rack to complete the cooling.

TOPPING In a medium-size bowl, combine and beat the sour cream, sugar, and vanilla until smooth. Spread the mixture evenly over the top of the cake and bake in a preheated 350° oven for 5 minutes. Remove the cake from the oven and place on a wire rack to cool. Carefully remove the sides of the spring-form pan and decorate the top by sprinkling on the walnuts. Transfer the cake to a serving dish and serve. For best results refrigerate for 2 hours before serving.

# Chocolate Cheesecakes

## TRADITIONAL CHOCOLATE CHEESECAKE

*The chocolate lover's dream cake, it may remind you of a very thick chocolate milkshake. You may want to add still another ounce of chocolate to make it even more "chocolatey." Be ready for friends' applause when you serve the Traditional Chocolate Cheesecake.*

CRUST
1½ cups chocolate wafer crumbs
¼ cup granulated sugar
2 tablespoons sweet butter, softened

FILLING
1½ ounces sweet baking chocolate
1 teaspoon sweet butter
1½ pounds cream cheese, softened
¾ cup granulated sugar
¼ cup heavy cream
¼ cup milk
2 eggs
¼ teaspoon salt
1½ teaspoons powdered sugar

PAN
9-inch springform pan

CRUST   In a small mixing bowl, combine the chocolate wafer crumbs, sugar, and butter. Blend well with fingers, fork, or pastry blender. Press or pat the mixture onto the bottom of a well-buttered springform pan. Chill in the freezer or refrigerator for about 30 minutes.

FILLING   In a double boiler, melt the chocolate completely with the butter. Meanwhile in a large bowl, beat the cream cheese, sugar, heavy cream, and milk. Add the eggs, one at a time, and beat until creamy and smooth. Add the melted chocolate and the salt and continue to beat until very smooth. Pour the mixture into the chilled pan. Place the springform pan inside of a larger pan containing 1 inch of water and bake in a preheated 325°F oven for 1½ hours. Transfer the cake to a wire rack, letting it cool completely. Carefully remove the sides of the springform pan and refrigerate the cake for about 2 hours. Sprinkle the top of the cake with the powdered sugar before serving.

# CHOCOLATE SWIRL
# CHEESECAKE

*This unique cheesecake, with its very attractive and tempting appearance, uses a chocolate graham cracker crust; a thick, extremely creamy cream cheese filling; and rich, unsweetened, pure cocoa generously swirled into the batter. A winning selection for any occasion.*

**CRUST**
1 cup graham cracker crumbs
¼ cup granulated sugar

2 tablespoons sweet butter, softened
3 tablespoons unsweetened cocoa

**FILLING**
1½ pounds cream cheese, softened
¾ cup granulated sugar
3 eggs
2 teaspoons vanilla extract
¼ teaspoon salt
½ cup sour cream

½ cup heavy cream
3 tablespoons unsweetened cocoa
2 to 3 tablespoons sweet butter
1½ teaspoons powdered sugar

**PAN**
9-inch springform pan

**CRUST** In a small mixing bowl, combine the graham cracker crumbs, sugar, and butter. Blend well with fingers, fork, or pastry blender. Next, with a spoon, mix in the cocoa. Press or pat the mixture onto the bottom of a well-buttered springform pan. Chill in the freezer or refrigerator for about 30 minutes.

**FILLING** In a large bowl, beat the cream cheese, sugar, and eggs until very smooth. Then add the vanilla, salt, sour cream, and heavy cream and continue to beat until very smooth and creamy. Pour the mixture into the chilled springform pan and let it stand while preparing the cocoa mixture. In a skillet, melt the butter, then blend in the cocoa, mixing well into a thick chocolate mixture. With a spoon, drop the cocoa mixture into the center of the cheese mixture, then with a knife swirl it around and around throughout the cheese mixture. Place the springform pan inside a larger pan containing 1 inch of water and bake in a preheated 325°F oven for 1½ hours. Transfer to a wire rack and allow to cool completely for about 3 hours. Carefully remove the sides of the springform pan and decorate the top of the cake with the powdered sugar or chocolate curls. Transfer to a serving dish and serve.

# MARBLE CHEESECAKE

*Another very popular cheesecake, this cake is made of a simple
graham cracker crust, with a light and creamy filling of
cream cheese and cottage cheese that is delicately flavored
with vanilla and lemon juice, and then marbleized with
unsweetened cocoa and topped with a light sprinkling of
powdered sugar. The aroma and appearance will entice your
guests to have extra-generous servings.*

**CRUST**
1 cup graham cracker
    crumbs
¼ cup granulated sugar

2 tablespoons sweet
    butter, softened

**FILLING**
1 pound cream cheese,
    softened
1 pound creamed cottage
    cheese
1 cup heavy cream
¼ pound (1 stick)
    sweet butter
½ cup granulated sugar
⅔ cup powdered sugar
6 eggs, separated

1 teaspoon lemon juice
rind of 1 lemon, grated
1 teaspoon vanilla extract
¼ cup all-purpose flour,
    sifted
¼ teaspoon salt
3 tablespoons
    unsweetened cocoa
1 tablespoon sweet butter

**PAN**
10-inch springform pan

**CRUST**   In a small mixing bowl, combine the graham cracker
crumbs, sugar, and butter. Blend well with fingers, fork, or pastry
blender. Press or pat the mixture onto the bottom of a well-
buttered springform pan. Chill in the freezer or refrigerator for
about 30 minutes.

**FILLING**   In a large bowl, beat the cream cheese, cottage cheese,
heavy cream, butter, and granulated sugar until very smooth

and creamy. Add ½ cup of the powdered sugar and the egg yolks and beat until smooth. In a small mixing bowl, beat the egg whites until stiff, then fold them into the cheese mixture. Add the lemon juice, grated lemon rind, vanilla, flour, and salt and beat well until smooth. In a small skillet, heat the cocoa and butter and mix until smooth. With a spoon, drop the cocoa mixture into the center of the cheese mixture, then with a knife swirl it around and around throughout the cheese mixture. Pour into the chilled pan and bake in a preheated 300°F oven for 1¾ hours. Then turn off the oven and allow to cool completely in the closed oven. Carefully remove the sides of the springform pan and decorate the top of the cake by sprinkling the remaining powdered sugar on it. Refrigerate until ready to serve.

# CHOCOLATE–MINT
# CHEESECAKE

*The aroma and flavor of mint, enhanced with chocolate, make this cake an unforgettable dining experience. An inspiration in place of the usual after-dinner mint. The bain-marie method will keep this cheesecake very moist and creamy. Let it cool completely before refrigerating, and allow it to return to room temperature before serving.*

**CRUST**
2¼ cups chocolate wafer crumbs
¼ cup granulated sugar
6 tablespoons (¾ stick) sweet butter, softened

**FILLING**
1½ pounds creamed cottage cheese
½ cup granulated sugar
2 eggs
½ cup light cream
1 teaspoon vanilla extract
½ teaspoon chocolate flavoring
3 tablespoons unsweetened cocoa

**TOPPING**
1½ cups sour cream
2 tablespoons crème de menthe
1 teaspoon mint extract
2 drops green food coloring
1 tablespoon granulated sugar
1 cup powdered sugar
1 tablespoon sweet butter, softened
1 tablespoon unsweetened cocoa
2 tablespoons milk
1 green cherry

**PAN**
9-inch springform pan

**CRUST** In a medium-size bowl, combine the chocolate wafer crumbs, sugar, and butter. Blend well with fingers, fork, or pastry blender. Press or pat the mixture onto the bottom and sides of a well-buttered springform pan. Chill in the freezer or refrigerator for about 30 minutes.

FILLING In a large bowl, beat the cottage cheese, sugar, and eggs until very smooth. Add the light cream, vanilla, chocolate flavoring, and cocoa and continue to beat until very smooth and creamy. Pour the mixture into the chilled pan. Place the spring-form pan inside of a larger pan containing 1 inch of water and bake in a preheated 325°F oven for 1½ hours. Transfer the cake to a wire rack and allow to cool for 30 minutes.

TOPPING In a large bowl, combine the sour cream, crème de menthe, mint extract, green food coloring, and sugar, then beat until very smooth. Spread the mixture evenly over the top of the cake and bake in a preheated 350° oven for 5 minutes. Transfer the cake to a wire rack and allow to cool thoroughly. Then re-move the sides of the springform pan and refrigerate the cake overnight.

After the cake has chilled overnight, prepare a chocolate glaze: In a small mixing bowl, combine powdered sugar and butter, then add the cocoa. Add the milk slowly to achieve spreading consistency, continuing to stir until smooth. Pour the chocolate glaze unevenly over the top of the cake. The glaze will set in 30 minutes. When the glaze is set, add the green cherry in the center of the cake. The cake may be either refrigerated for later use or served immediately.

# CHOCOLATE–ALMOND
# CHEESECAKE

*Chocolate wafers, toasted almonds, and a touch of Amaretto create a new dimension for the discerning palate. A very attractive cake—light and moist, not too sweet—it serves up to sixteen nicely. An excellent choice for a party.*

CRUST
1½ cups chocolate wafer crumbs
1 cup finely chopped blanched almonds, lightly toasted
⅓ cup granulated sugar
6 tablespoons (¾ stick) sweet butter, softened

FILLING
1½ pounds cream cheese, softened
1 cup granulated sugar
4 eggs
⅓ cup heavy cream
¼ cup Amaretto liqueur
1 teaspoon vanilla extract

TOPPING
1½ cups sour cream
1 tablespoon granulated sugar
1 teaspoon vanilla extract
1 cup slivered blanched almonds, lightly toasted

PAN
10-inch springform pan

CRUST   In a large bowl, combine the chocolate wafer crumbs, chopped almonds, sugar, and butter. Blend well with fingers, fork, or pastry blender. Press or pat the mixture onto the bottom and sides of a well-buttered springform pan. Chill in the freezer or refrigerator for 30 minutes.

FILLING   In a large bowl, beat the cream cheese, sugar, and eggs until smooth. Then add the heavy cream, Amaretto, and vanilla and continue to beat until very smooth. Pour the mixture into the chilled springform pan and bake in a preheated 375°F oven for 30 minutes. Transfer the cake to a wire rack and let stand until cool. Note: The cake will not be set.

**TOPPING** In a small mixing bowl, combine the sour cream, sugar, and vanilla and beat until smooth. Spread the mixture evenly over the top of the cake and bake in a preheated 375° oven for 5 minutes. Transfer the cake to a wire rack and let cool completely. Carefully remove the sides of the springform pan and press the slivered almonds around the top of the cake. Refrigerate overnight. Remove from the refrigerator at least 2 hours before serving.

---

# CHOCOLATE–RUM–RAISIN CHEESECAKE

*The blend of chocolate, rum, and raisin flavors in this cake will be dearly remembered by friends and guests. The plain chocolate topping can easily be decorated to suit any celebration.*

| | | |
|---|---|---|
| **CRUST** | 2¼ cups chocolate wafer crumbs<br>¼ cup granulated sugar | 6 tablespoons ( ¾ stick) sweet butter, softened |
| **FILLING** | 2 pounds cream cheese, softened<br>2 cups granulated sugar<br>2 teaspoons vanilla extract<br>5 eggs<br>3 cups sour cream | 1 tablespoon sweet butter<br>3 tablespoons unsweetened cocoa<br>¼ cup light rum<br>1 cup seedless raisins |
| **TOPPING** | 1½ cups sour cream<br>1 tablespoon granulated sugar | 1 tablespoon unsweetened cocoa |
| **PAN** | 10-inch springform pan | |

CRUST   In a medium-size bowl, combine the chocolate wafer crumbs, sugar, and butter. Blend well with fingers, fork, or pastry blender. Press or pat the mixture onto the bottom and sides of a well-buttered springform pan. Chill in the freezer or refrigerator for about 30 minutes.

FILLING   In a large bowl, beat the cream cheese, sugar, and vanilla until smooth. Add the eggs, one at a time, making sure that the mixture is well beaten after each addition. Fold in the sour cream, again making sure that the mixture is smooth. In a small skillet, melt the butter, add the cocoa, and blend well. Add the cocoa mixture, the rum, and the raisins to the cheese mixture and mix until smooth and creamy. Pour into the chilled pan and bake in a preheated 375°F oven for 1 hour, then turn off the oven, open the oven door 1 inch, and let the cake cool slowly for 1 hour.

TOPPING   In a small mixing bowl, beat the sour cream, sugar, and cocoa until very smooth, then spread the mixture evenly over the top of the cake and bake in a preheated 350° oven for 5 minutes. Transfer the cake to a wire rack and allow to cool completely. After cooling, carefully remove the sides of the springform pan and refrigerate the cake for 2 to 3 hours. Transfer the cake to a serving dish and serve.

# BLACK FOREST CHEESECAKE

*A most unusual recipe, with its chocolate wafer crust,*
*thick chocolate filling, and luscious cherry topping. A great idea*
*as a surprise dessert or for any festive occasion.*

CRUST | 2 cups chocolate wafer crumbs | 6 tablespoons ( ¾ stick ) sweet butter, softened
½ cup graham cracker crumbs | ¼ cup granulated sugar

FILLING | 1½ pounds cream cheese, softened | ½ teaspoon vanilla extract
½ cup granulated sugar | ¼ teaspoon salt
2 eggs | 2 cups cooked chocolate pudding mix

TOPPING | 21 ounces canned cherry pie filling and topping

PAN | 9-inch springform pan

CRUST   In a medium-size bowl, combine the chocolate wafer crumbs, graham cracker crumbs, butter, and sugar. Blend well with fingers, fork, or pastry blender. Press or pat the mixture onto the bottom and sides of a well-buttered springform pan. Chill in the freezer or refrigerator for 30 minutes.

FILLING   In a large bowl, beat the cream cheese and sugar until smooth. Add eggs, vanilla, and salt and beat again until smooth. In a medium-size saucepan, combine the chocolate pudding mix with the milk, and prepare according to package directions Add the chocolate pudding to the cheesecake mixture and beat until very smooth and creamy. Pour the mixture into the chilled pan. Place the springform pan inside of a larger pan containing 1 inch of water and bake in a preheated 325°F oven for 1½ hours.

Transfer the cake to a wire rack and let cool for at least 30 minutes. Note: The cake will not be set.

TOPPING   Spread the cherry pie filling evenly over the top of the cake and bake for another 15 minutes in a preheated 400° oven. Transfer the cake to wire rack, letting it cool completely. Refrigerate for 2 hours. Then remove the sides of the springform pan, but keep the cake in the refrigerator overnight. For best results, remove the cake from the refrigerator 2 hours before serving.

---

# Coffee
# Cheesecakes

## COFFEE CHEESECAKE

*For a nice change-of-pace dessert, try this smooth cake, generously flavored with coffee liqueur and freeze-dried instant coffee. Your favorite brew in cheesecake form, it's easy to prepare. Just sprinkle the top with powdered sugar or top it with whipped cream and a light dusting of cinnamon.*

**CAKE**
1½ pounds cream cheese, softened
1½ cups granulated sugar
1½ teaspoons vanilla extract
4 eggs
1 cup sour cream
1 cup heavy cream
1½ teaspoons coffee liqueur
1½ tablespoons freeze-dried instant coffee, dissolved in 2 tablespoons of water
1½ teaspoons powdered sugar

**PAN**
10-inch springform pan

In a large bowl, beat the cream cheese, sugar, vanilla, and eggs until very smooth. Add the sour cream, heavy cream, and coffee liqueur and continue to beat until very smooth and creamy. Add the coffee paste to the cheese mixture and beat until smooth. Pour into a well-buttered springform pan and bake in a preheated 350°F oven for 1¼ hours. When done, turn off the oven and allow the cake to cool in the open oven for 1 hour. Transfer

to a wire rack and allow to cool completely. Carefully remove
the sides of the springform pan, transfer to a serving dish, and
decorate the top of the cake with the powdered sugar. Either
serve immediately or refrigerate.

---

# IRISH COFFEE CHEESECAKE

*Imagine a variation of Irish coffee and cheesecake combined
in a delicate pastry shell. This cake consists of a smooth,
light cottage cheese filling, flavored with coffee liqueur,
Irish Mist liqueur, and freeze-dried coffee, and is topped with
a mound of freshly whipped cream. Serve this in place of
the customary after-dinner cordial.*

SHELL
1½ cups all-purpose flour, sifted
¼ cup granulated sugar
¼ pound (1 stick) sweet butter, softened
1 egg

FILLING
2 pounds creamed cottage cheese
2 eggs, separated
2 tablespoons granulated sugar
1 tablespoon sweet butter, melted
1 teaspoon vanilla extract
⅛ teaspoon cream of tartar
1 teaspoon coffee liqueur
1½ tablespoons Irish Mist liqueur
2 tablespoons water
2 tablespoons freeze-dried instant coffee

TOPPING
1 cup heavy cream, whipped

PAN
9-inch springform pan

SHELL   In a large bowl, combine the flour, sugar, butter, and
egg. Blend well with fingers, fork, or pastry blender. Form the
dough into a ball, knead lightly with the heel of the hand against

a smooth surface for a few seconds, then reform it into a ball. Wrap it in wax paper and chill in the refrigerator for 1 hour. When chilled, roll out the dough on a floured surface until ⅛ inch thick. Fit the dough into the springform pan, pressing it 2 inches up the sides of the pan and crimping the edge decoratively. Prick the bottom of the shell with a fork and chill in the freezer or refrigerator for 30 minutes. Next, line the shell with wax paper, fill it with uncooked rice or dried beans, and bake it in a preheated 350°F oven for 10 minutes. Carefully remove the rice and wax paper and bake the shell for another 10 minutes. Transfer to a wire rack and allow to cool for about 30 minutes.

FILLING In a large bowl, beat the cottage cheese, egg yolks, and sugar until smooth. Add the melted butter and vanilla and continue to beat until smooth. In a small mixing bowl, beat the egg whites and cream of tartar until the whites hold their peaks. Fold them into the cottage cheese mixture. In a small skillet, heat the water and mix in the instant coffee until it becomes a thick paste, then add the coffee liqueur and Irish Mist and stir until smooth. Add the coffee mixture to the cheese mixture and combine gently until very smooth. Pour into the cooled pan and bake in a preheated 350° oven for 45 minutes. Transfer to a wire rack and allow to cool completely.

TOPPING Carefully remove the sides of the springform pan and decorate the top of the cake by spreading the whipped cream over it. Transfer to a serving dish and either serve immediately or refrigerate.

# Cheesecakes
# with
# Fruit

## COUNTRY-STYLE APPLE
## CHEESECAKE

*Good old apple pie in cheesecake form. A light pie crust with a layer of apple pie filling, covered by a creamy cheesecake mix, then topped with more apple pie filling and a dash of cinnamon. The bouquet of apples and cinnamon will arouse appetities.*

**SHELL**
1½ cups all-purpose flour, sifted
¼ cup granulated sugar
¼ pound (1 stick) sweet butter, softened
1 egg

**FILLING**
1½ pounds cream cheese, softened
½ cup granulated sugar
3 eggs
1 cup heavy cream
1 teaspoon lemon juice
1 cup canned apple pie filling and topping

**TOPPING**
21 ounces canned apple pie filling and topping
½ teaspoon ground cinnamon

**PAN**
9-inch springform pan

**SHELL**  In a large bowl, combine the flour, sugar, butter, and egg. Blend well with fingers, fork, or pastry blender. Form the dough into a ball, knead lightly with heel of the hand against a smooth surface for a few seconds, then reform it into a ball. Wrap it in wax paper and chill in the refrigerator for 1 hour. When chilled, roll out the dough on a floured surface until ⅛ inch thick. Fit the dough into the springform pan, pressing it 2 inches up the sides of the pan and crimping the edge decoratively. Prick the bottom of the shell with a fork and chill in the freezer or refrigerator for 30 minutes. Next, line the shell with wax paper, fill it with uncooked rice or dried beans, and bake it in a preheated 350°F oven for 10 minutes. Carefully remove the rice and wax paper and return the shell to the oven for another 10 minutes. Transfer the pan to a wire rack and allow to cool completely.

FILLING   In a large bowl, beat the cream cheese, sugar, and eggs until very smooth. Add the heavy cream and lemon juice and continue to beat until smooth. Fold in the apple pie filling. Pour the mixture into the cooled shell and bake in a preheated 350° oven for 1 hour. Transfer the cake to a wire rack and let cool completely.

TOPPING   Spread the apple pie filling evenly over the top of the cake and sprinkle the cinnamon on top of it. Bake in a preheated 400° oven for 15 minutes. Transfer the cake to a wire rack and let cool completely. Remove the sides of the springform pan and refrigerate for 2 hours. Remove from the refrigerator, transfer the cake to a serving dish, and serve.

# APPLE AND RAISIN CHEESECAKE

*A fall-winter favorite, apples and raisins blend into a light and creamy batter of cream cheese, heavy cream, and sour cream, with a sour cream topping garnished with cinnamon sugar and chopped walnuts. The perfect complement to after-dinner coffee.*

**CRUST**
2¼ cups graham cracker crumbs
¼ cup granulated sugar
¼ teaspoon ground cinnamon
6 tablespoons (¾ stick) sweet butter, softened

**FILLING**
1½ pounds cream cheese, softened
¾ cup granulated sugar
3 eggs
1 teaspoon vanilla extract
½ cup heavy cream
½ cup sour cream
½ cup seedless raisins
1 cup canned apple pie filling and topping

**TOPPING**
1½ cups sour cream
2 tablespoons granulated cinnamon sugar
½ cup finely chopped walnuts

**PAN**
9-inch springform pan

**CRUST**  In a medium-size bowl, combine the graham cracker crumbs, sugar, cinnamon, and butter. Blend well with fingers, fork, or pastry blender. Press or pat the mixture onto the bottom and sides of a well-buttered springform pan. Chill in the freezer or refrigerator for 30 minutes.

**FILLING**  In a large bowl, beat the cream cheese, sugar, and eggs until very smooth. Add the vanilla, heavy cream, and sour cream and continue to beat until smooth. Fold in the raisins and apple pie filling. Pour the mixture into the chilled pan. Place the springform pan inside of a larger pan containing 1 inch of water and bake in a preheated 350°F oven for 1½ hours. Transfer the cake to a wire rack and allow to cool for 30 minutes.

**TOPPING** In a small mixing bowl, beat the sour cream and cinnamon sugar until smooth. Spread the mixture evenly over the top of the cake and bake in a preheated 350° oven for 5 minutes. Transfer the cake to a wire rack and allow to cool completely. Carefully remove the sides of the springform pan and decorate the top of the cake with chopped walnuts. Transfer to a serving dish and either serve immediately or refrigerate.

---

# APRICOT–ALMOND CHEESECAKE

*Uniting apricot and almond flavors with cream cheese and ricotta cheese results in this extraordinary cheesecake, recalling the taste of apricot-filled pastry. This cake is best when served at room temperature.*

| | | |
|---|---|---|
| **CRUST** | 1¾ cups vanilla wafer crumbs | ¼ cup granulated sugar |
| | ½ cup finely chopped almonds | 6 tablespoons (¾ stick) sweet butter, softened |
| **FILLING** | 1 pound cream cheese, softened | ½ cup heavy cream |
| | 1 pound ricotta cheese | ⅛ teaspoon salt |
| | ¾ cup granulated sugar | 1½ teaspoons almond extract |
| | 3 eggs | 1 teaspoon apricot brandy |
| **TOPPING** | 1 cup apricot preserve | 1 cup finely sliced almonds |
| **PAN** | 9-inch springform pan | |

CRUST  In a medium-size bowl, combine the vanilla wafer crumbs, chopped almonds, sugar, and butter. Blend well with fingers, fork, or pastry blender. Press or pat the mixture onto the bottom and sides of a well-buttered springform pan. Chill in the freezer or refrigerator for approximately 30 minutes.

FILLING  In a large bowl, beat the cream cheese, ricotta cheese, sugar, and eggs until smooth. Add the heavy cream, salt, almond extract, and apricot brandy and continue to beat until very smooth and creamy. Pour into the chilled pan. Place the springform pan inside of a larger pan containing 1 inch of water and bake in a preheated 325°F oven for 1½ hours. Transfer the cake to a wire rack and allow to cool completely.

TOPPING  Spread the apricot preserve evenly over the top of the cake and decorate with sliced almonds. Carefully remove the sides of the springform pan and transfer the cake to a serving dish. Refrigerate for 2 hours before serving.

# APRICOT–AMARETTINI CHEESECAKE

*This calls for using Amarettini di Saronno cookies (almond macaroons) in the crust and sprinkled over the topping of apricot preserves and apricot slices—resulting in a distinctive dessert that will win the praise of friends and family.*

| | | |
|---|---|---|
| **CRUST** | 2 cups Amarettini di Saronno cookie crumbs<br>¼ cup finely chopped almonds | ¼ cup granulated sugar<br>6 tablespoons (¾ stick) sweet butter, softened |
| **FILLING** | 1½ pounds cream cheese, softened<br>½ cup granulated sugar<br>3 eggs | 1 teaspoon almond extract<br>½ cup heavy cream<br>½ cup sour cream |
| **TOPPING** | 1 cup apricot preserve<br>1 cup canned apricots, drained and sliced | ¼ cup finely crushed Amarettini di Saronno cookies |
| **PAN** | 9-inch springform pan | |

**CRUST** In a medium-size bowl, combine the cookie crumbs, chopped almonds, sugar, and butter. Blend well with fingers, fork, or pastry blender. Press or pat the mixture onto the bottom and sides of a well-buttered springform pan. Chill in the freezer or refrigerator for approximately 30 minutes.

**FILLING** In a large bowl, beat the cream cheese, sugar, and eggs until smooth. Add the almond extract, heavy cream, and sour cream and continue to beat until very smooth and creamy. Pour the mixture into the chilled pan. Place the springform pan inside of a larger pan containing 1 inch of water and bake in a preheated 325°F oven for 1½ hours. Transfer the cake to a wire rack and allow to cool completely.

**TOPPING** Spread the apricot preserve evenly over the top of the cake and decorate the outer edge with the sliced apricots. Sprinkle the crushed cookies in the center of the cake. Carefully remove the sides of the springform pan and transfer the cake to a serving dish. Refrigerate for at least 2 hours before serving.

---

# APRICOT AND PEACH
# CHEESECAKE

*An apricot cheesecake making use of both apricot puree and nectar as the main flavoring ingredients, and a topping of fresh or canned sliced peaches, to yield an interesting marriage of the two fruit flavors—truly a gourmet's delight.*

| | | |
|---|---|---|
| **SHELL** | 1½ cups all-purpose flour, sifted | ¼ pound (1 stick) sweet butter, softened |
| | ¼ cup granulated sugar | 1 egg |
| **FILLING** | 1 cup canned apricot puree | 3 eggs |
| | 1½ pounds cream cheese, softened | 1 cup heavy cream |
| | ¾ cup granulated sugar | 1 teaspoon vanilla extract |
| | | 1 tablespoon apricot nectar |
| **TOPPING** | 1½ cups sour cream | 1½ cups canned sliced peaches, drained (or fresh peaches, if in season) |
| | 2 tablespoons granulated sugar | |
| **PAN** | 9-inch springform pan | |

SHELL In a large bowl, combine the flour, sugar, butter, and egg. Blend well with fingers, fork, or pastry blender. Form the dough into a ball, knead lightly with the heel of the hand against a smooth surface for a few seconds, then reform it into a ball. Wrap it in wax paper and chill in the refrigerator for 1 hour. When chilled, roll out the dough on a floured surface until ⅛ inch thick. Fit the dough into the springform pan, pressing it 2 inches up the sides of the pan and crimping the edge decoratively. Prick the bottom of the shell with a fork and chill in the freezer or refrigerator for about 30 minutes. Next, line the shell with wax paper, fill it with rice, and bake it in a preheated 350°F oven for 10 minutes. Carefully remove the rice and wax paper and return the shell to the oven for another 10 minutes. Transfer the pan to a wire rack and allow to cool completely. Pour the apricot puree onto the bottom of the cooled shell and place in the refrigerator or freezer for 15 minutes.

FILLING In a large bowl, beat the cream cheese, sugar, and eggs until very smooth. Add the heavy cream, vanilla, and apricot nectar and beat until very smooth and creamy. Pour the mixture into the chilled shell over the apricot puree and bake in a preheated 350° oven for 1¼ hours. Transfer the cake to a wire rack and allow to cool for 30 minutes.

TOPPING In a small mixing bowl, beat the sour cream and sugar until smooth, then spread the mixture evenly over the top of the cake and bake in a preheated 350° oven for 5 minutes. Transfer the cake to a wire rack and let cool. Remove the sides of the springform pan and decorate the top of the cake with the sliced peaches. Transfer the cake to a serving dish and serve. Note: It is preferable (but not absolutely necessary) to refrigerate the cake overnight and then remove the cake from the refrigerator at least 2 hours before it is to be served.

# BANANA CHEESECAKE

*Combined flavors of grainy banana and walnut, enhanced by a
hint of cinnamon and blended into a rich cream cheese mixture,
create a very appealing cheesecake. Remember to add a drop
of lemon juice to the sliced bananas to prevent their darkening.
Try this when you want a sweet but subtle dessert.*

CRUST
1¾ cups vanilla wafer
crumbs
¼ cup granulated sugar

¼ cup finely chopped
walnuts
6 tablespoons (¾ stick)
sweet butter, softened

FILLING
1½ pounds cream cheese,
softened
½ cup granulated sugar
2 eggs
1 teaspoon vanilla extract

1½ teaspoons banana
liqueur
¼ cup heavy cream
¼ cup milk
2 bananas, sliced
crosswise

TOPPING
1½ cups sour cream
1 tablespoon granulated
sugar
a few drops of lemon
juice

2 bananas, sliced into ¼-
inch crosswise slices
½ teaspoon ground
cinnamon

PAN
9-inch springform pan

CRUST   In a medium-size bowl, combine the vanilla wafer
crumbs, sugar, chopped walnuts, and butter. Blend well with
fingers, fork, or pastry blender. Press or pat the mixture onto the
bottom and sides of a well-buttered springform pan and chill
in the freezer or refrigerator for about 30 minutes.

FILLING   In a large bowl, beat the cream cheese, sugar, and eggs
until smooth. Add the vanilla, banana liqueur, heavy cream, and

milk and beat until very smooth and creamy. With a spoon, fold
in the banana slices. Pour the mixture into the chilled pan. Place
the springform pan inside of a larger pan containing 1 inch of
water and bake in a preheated 325°F oven for 1½ hours. Transfer the cake to a wire rack and allow to cool for 30 minutes.

TOPPING   In a small mixing bowl, beat the sour cream and sugar
until very smooth. Spread the mixture evenly over the top of the
cake and bake in a preheated 350° oven for 5 minutes. Transfer
the cake to a wire rack and allow to cool completely. Carefully
remove the sides of the springform pan and decorate the cake
with the sliced bananas which have been brushed lightly with a
few drops of lemon juice, sprinkling the cinnamon over the
banana slices. Refrigerate overnight. Remove the cake from the
refrigerator at least 1 hour before serving. (You may prefer to
wait to prepare this topping until just before serving; this will
ensure the freshness of the bananas and reduce the risk of their
discoloring.)

# BLUEBERRY CHEESECAKE

*A fabulous cheesecake, delicate and creamy, with lots of blueberries evenly diffused throughout the batter in blueberry-muffin fashion. Sprinkle the top with powdered sugar, or top with a blueberry pie filling.*

**CAKE**

2 pounds cream cheese, softened
½ cup heavy cream
6 eggs
1½ cups granulated sugar
3 tablespoons cornstarch
3 tablespoons flour
1½ tablespoons vanilla extract

2 tablespoons lemon juice
1 cup sour cream
¼ pound (1 stick) sweet butter, melted
1¾ cups fresh blueberries
1½ teaspoons powdered sugar

**PAN**     9-inch springform pan

In a large bowl, beat the cream cheese, heavy cream, eggs, sugar, cornstarch, flour, vanilla, and lemon juice. Blend in the sour cream, butter, and blueberries. Pour the mixture into a well-buttered springform pan and bake in a preheated 350°F oven for 1 hour, then open the oven door and let cool for 1 hour in the open oven. Refrigerate overnight. Carefully remove the sides of the springform pan and decorate the cake by sprinkling the top with the powdered sugar. For best results, let the cake stand at room temperature for 2 hours before serving.

# CAPE COD BLUEBERRY CHEESECAKE

*A light and very creamy cheesecake with ground hazelnuts in the crust, brandy extract in the filling, and a topping of mildly tart blueberries. An ideal dessert to serve fruit fanciers when the berries are in season.*

| | | |
|---|---|---|
| **CRUST** | 1 cup vanilla wafer crumbs | 3 tablespoons granulated sugar |
| | ¾ cup finely ground hazelnuts | 3 tablespoons sweet butter, softened |
| **FILLING** | 1 pound cream cheese, softened | 1 teaspoon brandy extract |
| | 1 cup granulated sugar | 2 tablespoons all-purpose flour, sifted |
| | 4 eggs, separated | ¼ teaspoon salt |
| | 1 cup sour cream | |
| **TOPPING** | 2 cups fresh blueberries | 1 teaspoon water |
| | 2 tablespoons cornstarch | ½ teaspoon brandy extract |
| | 2 tablespoons granulated sugar | ½ teaspoon lemon juice |
| **PAN** | 9-inch springform pan | |

**CRUST** In a small mixing bowl, combine the vanilla wafer crumbs, ground hazelnuts, sugar, and butter. Blend well with fingers, fork, or pastry blender. Press or pat the mixture onto the bottom and sides of a well-buttered springform pan. Chill in the freezer or refrigerator for approximately 30 minutes.

**FILLING** In a large bowl, beat the cream cheese, sugar, and egg yolks until very smooth. Add the sour cream and brandy extract and continue to beat until smooth. Add the flour and salt and mix well. In a separate small mixing bowl, beat the egg whites until stiff, then fold them into the cheese mixture until smooth. Pour into the chilled pan and bake in a preheated 350°F oven for 1 hour. Turn off the oven and let the cake remain in the closed oven until completely cooled.

TOPPING   In a large saucepan, mix the blueberries, cornstarch, sugar, and water and bring to a boil, then stir over medium heat for 3 to 5 minutes, until thick and smooth. Add the brandy extract and lemon juice, stirring well. Remove from the heat. Spread the blueberry mixture evenly over the top of the cake and refrigerate for about 5 to 6 hours. Carefully remove the sides of the springform pan, transfer the cake to a serving dish, and serve.

---

# NEW ENGLAND BLUEBERRY CHEESECAKE

*With the surprise of a layer of blueberries at the bottom and blueberry pie filling on top, this one will especially please your children as a treat.*

| | | |
|---|---|---|
| CRUST | 2¼ cups vanilla wafer crumbs | 6 tablespoons ( ¾ stick) sweet butter, softened |
| | ¼ cup granulated sugar | 1 cup fresh blueberries |
| FILLING | 1½ pounds cream cheese, softened | 1 tablespoon vanilla extract |
| | ¾ cup granulated sugar | ½ cup heavy cream |
| | 3 eggs | |
| TOPPING | 1½ cups canned blueberry pie filling and topping | |
| PAN | 9-inch springform pan | |

CRUST In a medium-size bowl, combine the vanilla wafer crumbs, sugar, and butter. Blend well with fingers, fork, or pastry blender. Press or pat the mixture onto the bottom and sides of a well-buttered springform pan. Pour the blueberries onto the bottom of the crust, then chill in the freezer or refrigerator for about 30 minutes.

FILLING In a large bowl, beat the cream cheese, sugar, and eggs until very smooth. Add the vanilla and heavy cream and continue to beat until smooth. Pour into the chilled pan. Place the springform pan inside of a larger pan containing 1 inch of water and bake in a preheated 325°F oven for 1½ hours. Transfer the cake to a wire rack and allow to cool for 30 minutes.

TOPPING Spread the blueberry pie filling and topping evenly over the top of the cake and bake in a preheated 400° oven for 15 minutes. Transfer to a wire rack and let cool completely. Carefully remove the sides of the springform pan and refrigerate the cake overnight. Remove from the refrigerator at least 2 hours before serving.

# CHERRY CHEESECAKE

*The long-popular Cherry Cheesecake: a simple graham cracker crust; an extremely light, moist, creamy filling; and a generous layer of cherry pie filling on top—and oh so easy to make.*

| | | |
|---|---|---|
| **CRUST** | 1¼ cups graham cracker crumbs | ¼ pound (1 stick) sweet butter, softened |
| | ½ teaspoon ground cinnamon | |
| **FILLING** | 1 pound cream cheese, softened | ¼ teaspoon salt |
| | 3 eggs | 2 teaspoons vanilla extract |
| | 1 cup granulated sugar | 1 teaspoon almond extract |
| | | 3 cups sour cream |
| **TOPPING** | 21 ounces canned cherry pie filling and topping | |
| **PAN** | 9-inch springform pan | |

**CRUST**  In a small mixing bowl, combine the graham cracker crumbs, cinnamon, and butter. Blend well with fingers, fork, or pastry blender. Press or pat the mixture onto the bottom of a well-buttered springform pan. Chill in the freezer or refrigerator for about 30 minutes.

**FILLING**  In a large bowl, beat the cream cheese, eggs, sugar, salt, vanilla, and almond extract until smooth. Fold in the sour cream and beat until very smooth. Pour the mixture into the chilled pan and refrigerate for 1 hour. When chilled, bake in a preheated 375°F oven for 45 minutes. Transfer to a wire rack to cool, then refrigerate for 6 hours.

**TOPPING**  Spread the cherry pie filling over the top of the cake very evenly, then bake in a preheated 400° oven for 15 minutes.

Transfer to a wire rack and allow to cool thoroughly. Carefully remove the sides of the springform pan and refrigerate overnight. Remove the cake from the refrigerator at least 2 hours before serving.

---

# NEW ORLEANS CHERRY CHEESECAKE

*A luxuriant cheesecake that is reminiscent of French Quarter dining. The delicate blend of dark, sweet cherries and Grand Marnier orange liqueur in this light and creamy cheesecake, topped with whipped cream and chopped walnuts, will delight the most knowing of cheesecake connoisseurs.*

**SHELL**
1½ cups all-purpose flour, sifted
¼ cup granulated sugar
¼ pound (1 stick) butter, softened
1 egg

**FILLING**
2½ pounds cream cheese, softened
1¾ cups granulated sugar
6 eggs
¼ cup heavy cream
3 tablespoons all-purpose flour, sifted
1 tablespoon lemon juice
1 tablespoon vanilla extract
1½ tablespoons Grand Marnier
1 cup canned, pitted, dark sweet cherries, drained

**TOPPING**
1 cup heavy cream
½ cup chopped walnuts

**PAN**
10-inch springform pan

**SHELL** In a large bowl, combine the flour, sugar, butter, and egg. Blend well with fingers, fork, or pastry blender. Form the dough into a ball, knead lightly with the heel of the hand against a

smooth surface for a few seconds, then reform it into a ball.
Wrap it in wax paper and chill in the refrigerator for 1 hour.
When chilled, roll out the dough on a floured surface until ⅛
inch thick. Fit the dough into the springform pan, pressing it
2 inches up the sides of the pan and crimping the edge decoratively. Prick the bottom of the shell with a fork and chill for
1 hour.

FILLING   In a large bowl, beat the cream cheese, sugar, and eggs
until smooth. Add the heavy cream, flour, lemon juice, vanilla,
and Grand Marnier and continue to beat until smooth and
creamy. Pour the mixture into the chilled pan. Distribute the
cherries on top of the mixture and press them into the mixture
with a spatula until all are covered. Bake in a preheated 450°F
oven for 30 minutes, then reduce the temperature to 250° and
continue to bake for 1¼ hours longer. Transfer the cake to a
wire rack and allow to cool completely.

TOPPING   In a chilled small mixing bowl, beat or whip the heavy
cream until the peaks are stiff, then spread the whipped cream
over the top of the cake and sprinkle the chopped walnuts over
the cream. Transfer the cake to a serving plate and serve.

# BLACK CHERRY CHEESECAKE

*Black cherries floating in a rich, creamy cheesecake,
with a sour cream topping and chopped nuts, all bring to mind
a cherry vanilla ice-cream sundae. Surprise the family with
cheesecake instead of ice cream for dessert.*

CRUST
- 1¾ cups vanilla wafer crumbs
- ¼ cup granulated sugar
- ¼ cup finely chopped mixed nuts (walnuts, peanuts, hazelnuts, or cashews)
- 6 tablespoons (¾ stick) sweet butter, softened

FILLING
- 1½ pounds cream cheese, softened
- ½ cup granulated sugar
- 2 eggs
- 1½ teaspoons vanilla extract
- ½ cup light cream
- 2 cups canned sweetened, pitted black cherries, drained

TOPPING
- 1½ cups sour cream
- 1 tablespoon granulated sugar
- 1 black cherry
- ¼ cup chopped mixed nuts

PAN  9-inch springform pan

CRUST In a medium-size bowl, combine the vanilla wafer crumbs, sugar, chopped mixed nuts, and butter. Blend well with fingers, fork, or pastry blender. Press or pat the mixture onto the bottom and sides of a well-buttered springform pan. Chill in the freezer or refrigerator for about 30 minutes.

FILLING In a large bowl, beat the cream cheese, sugar, and eggs until smooth. Add the vanilla and light cream and beat until very smooth and fairly thick. Fold in the black cherries. Pour the mixture into the chilled pan. Place the springform pan inside of a larger pan containing 1 inch of water and bake in a preheated

325°F oven for 1½ hours. Transfer the cake to a wire rack and allow to cool for about 30 minutes.

TOPPING   In a small mixing bowl, beat the sour cream and sugar until smooth. Spread the mixture evenly over the top of the cake and bake in a preheated 350° oven for 5 minutes. Transfer the cake to a wire rack and allow to cool for about 2 to 3 hours. Remove the sides of the springform pan and decorate the top of the cake with the black cherry and chopped nuts. Refrigerate overnight. Remove the cake from the refrigerator at least 2 hours before serving.

---

# CHERRY–PECAN CHEESECAKE

*The cherry-pecan connection—a combination to delight the palate: a vanilla wafer crust; a light, smooth cream cheese filling in which whole pecans and glacéed cherries are diffused; and a topping of sour cream that has been creatively decorated with cherries and pecans.*

CRUST
: 1 cup vanilla wafer crumbs
: ¼ cup granulated sugar
: 2 tablespoons sweet butter, softened

FILLING
: 2 pounds cream cheese, softened
: 2 cups granulated sugar
: 2 pints sour cream
: 1 teaspoon salt
: 2 tablespoons cornstarch
: 6 eggs
: 1 cup whole pecans
: ½ cup glacéed cherries

TOPPING
: 1½ cups sour cream
: 1 tablespoon granulated sugar
: ½ cup whole pecans
: ¼ cup glacéed cherries

PAN
: 10-inch springform pan

CRUST  In a small mixing bowl, combine the vanilla wafer crumbs, sugar, and butter. Blend well with fingers, fork, or pastry blender. Press or pat the mixture onto the bottom of a well-buttered springform pan. Chill in the freezer or refrigerator for about 30 minutes.

FILLING  In a large bowl, beat the cream cheese, sugar, sour cream, and salt until very smooth and creamy. Add the cornstarch and eggs, one at a time, beating well after each addition. Fold in the pecans and glacéed cherries. Pour the mixture into the chilled pan and bake in a preheated 375°F oven for 1 hour. Then turn off the oven and allow to cool in the closed oven for an additional hour.

TOPPING  In a small mixing bowl, beat the sour cream and sugar until very smooth, then spread the mixture evenly over the top of the cake and bake in a preheated 350° oven for 5 minutes. Transfer to a wire rack and allow to cool completely. Remove the sides of the springform pan and decorate the top of the cake with the pecans and glacéed cherries. Transfer to a serving dish and refrigerate for at least 2 hours before serving.

# CRANBERRY CHEESECAKE

*Attractive and colorful, this dessert is a natural for Thanksgiving and Christmas entertaining. The delicate aroma and taste of orange and lemon rinds in the crust, the subtle blend of vanilla and orange extracts in the filling, and the layer of fresh cranberries for the topping combine to make this the grand finale to a holiday dinner.*

**SHELL**
1 cup all-purpose flour, sifted
¼ cup granulated sugar
¼ pound (1 stick) sweet butter, softened
1 teaspoon grated orange rind
1 teaspoon grated lemon rind
¼ teaspoon vanilla extract

**FILLING**
2½ pounds cream cheese, softened
1¾ cups granulated sugar
3 tablespoons all-purpose flour, sifted
1 teaspoon grated orange rind
½ teaspoon vanilla extract
½ teaspoon orange extract
⅛ teaspoon salt
5 whole eggs
2 egg yolks
¼ cup heavy cream

**TOPPING**
2 cups fresh cranberries
1¼ cups granulated sugar
½ cup water
1 tablespoon cornstarch, dissolved in 2 tablespoons water

**PAN**     10-inch springform pan

**SHELL**   In a large bowl, combine the flour, sugar, butter, grated orange and lemon rinds, and vanilla. Blend well with fingers, fork, or pastry blender. Form the dough into a ball, knead lightly with the heel of the hand against a smooth surface for about 15 seconds, then reform it into a ball. Wrap it in wax paper and chill in the refrigerator for about 1 hour. When chilled, roll out the dough on a floured surface until ⅛ inch thick. Fit the dough into a well-buttered springform pan, pressing it 2 inches up the sides of the pan and crimping the edge decoratively. Chill in the freezer or refrigerator for about 30 minutes.

FILLING  In a large bowl, beat the cream cheese, sugar, flour, grated orange rind, vanilla, orange extract, and salt until very smooth and creamy. Add the whole eggs and egg yolks, one at a time, beating well after each addition. Stir in the heavy cream. Pour the mixture into the chilled shell and bake in a preheated 450°F oven for 15 minutes, then reduce the temperature to 300° and continue to bake for 1 hour. Transfer the cake to a wire rack and allow to cool for 30 minutes.

TOPPING  In a large saucepan, combine the cranberries, sugar, and water, bring it to a boil, then let simmer for 3 minutes. Add the cornstarch-water mixture and stir to a very smooth consistency. Remove from the heat and continue stirring for 1 to 2 minutes until smooth and thick. Let the mixture cool, then spread it evenly over the top of the cake and refrigerate for at least 2 hours. Carefully remove the sides of the springform pan, transfer the cake to a serving dish, and serve.

# TROPICAL KIWI CHEESECAKE

*A rare gem of a cheesecake, with its delicate green topping
of sliced kiwis and the incomparable flavor of strawberries—
truly an artistic and delicious dessert to serve guests. They will
surely want generous portions once they glimpse this one.*

**SHELL**
1½ cups all-purpose flour, sifted
¼ cup granulated sugar

¼ pound (1 stick) sweet butter, softened
1 egg

**FILLING**
2 pounds skim-milk ricotta cheese
½ cup granulated sugar
3 egg yolks
1 whole egg
1 cup heavy cream

¼ cup finely ground hazelnuts
2 tablespoons light rum
2 tablespoons lemon juice
⅛ teaspoon salt

**TOPPING**
½ cup light honey
1 teaspoon lemon juice

4 ripe kiwis

**PAN**
9-inch springform pan

**SHELL**   In a large bowl, combine the flour, sugar, butter, and egg. Blend well with fingers, fork, or pastry blender. Form the dough into a ball, knead lightly with the heel of the hand against a smooth surface for a few seconds, then reform it into a ball. Wrap it in wax paper and chill in the refrigerator for 1 hour. When chilled, roll out the dough on a floured surface until ⅛ inch thick. Fit the dough into the springform pan, pressing it 2 inches up the sides of the pan and crimping the edge decoratively. Prick the bottom of the shell with a fork and chill in the freezer or refrigerator for 30 minutes. Next, line the shell with wax paper, fill it with uncooked rice or dried beans, and bake it in a preheated 350°F oven for 10 minutes. Carefully remove the rice and wax paper and return the shell to the oven for another 10 to 15 minutes. Transfer the pan to a wire rack and allow to cool completely.

FILLING In a large bowl, beat the ricotta cheese, sugar, and egg yolks until very smooth. Add the whole egg, heavy cream, hazel-nuts, rum, lemon juice, and salt and continue to beat until very smooth and creamy. Pour the mixture into the cooled shell and bake in a preheated 350° oven for 1 hour. Transfer the cake to a wire rack and let cool thoroughly. Carefully remove the sides of the springform pan and transfer the cake to a serving dish.

TOPPING In a small mixing bowl, combine the honey and lemon juice. Peel the kiwis, then halve them lengthwise and cut again crosswise into ¼-inch slices. Arrange the Kiwi slices decoratively on top of the cake, and just before serving, brush them with the honey to form a glaze. For best results, refrigerate overnight, and then remove from the refrigerator at least 2 hours before serving.

# ORANGE CHEESECAKE

*This is a most attractive, inviting cheesecake, with its graham cracker crust, and light and smooth cream cheese filling, gently flavored with orange rind and topped with an orange glaze. It's superb when creatively decorated with mandarin orange slices.*

**CRUST**
1 cup graham cracker
  crumbs
3 tablespoons granulated
  sugar
3 tablespoons sweet
  butter, softened

**FILLING**
1 pound cream cheese,
  softened
4 tablespoons ( ½ stick )
  sweet butter
½ cup granulated sugar
¼ cup flour
2 eggs
1 cup milk
1½ teaspoons vanilla
  extract
1 teaspoon grated orange
  rind

**TOPPING**
¼ cup granulated sugar
1 tablespoon cornstarch
½ cup orange juice
¼ cup water
½ cup canned mandarin
  orange slices, drained

**PAN**     10-inch springform pan

**CRUST**  In a small mixing bowl, combine the graham cracker crumbs, sugar, and butter. Blend well with fingers, fork, or pastry blender. Press or pat onto the bottom of a well-buttered springform pan. Bake in a preheated 325°F oven for 10 minutes, then remove from the oven and allow to cool on a wire rack for at least 15 minutes.

**FILLING**  In a large bowl, beat the cream cheese, butter, sugar, and flour, then add the eggs, one at a time, mixing well after each addition. Blend in the milk, vanilla, and grated orange rind and beat until smooth and creamy. Pour the mixture over the baked crust and bake in a preheated 350° oven for 30 minutes. Transfer to a wire rack to cool completely.

TOPPING In a small saucepan, combine the sugar, cornstarch, orange juice, and water and cook for 3 minutes, until clear and thick, stirring occasionally, Let cool, then spoon over the top of the cake. Chill for 30 minutes or until the icing is set. Carefully remove the sides of the springform pan and decorate the top of the cake with the mandarin orange slices. Refrigerate overnight. Remove from the refrigerator at least 2 hours before serving.

---

# PEACH CHEESECAKE

*Cottage cheese, peaches, and chopped pecans will awaken taste buds when served in the form of this cheesecake. Decorate the top by carefully placing peach slices one-by-one around the outer edge of the cake. Serve generous portions with coffee to your guests, and relish their delight.*

| | | |
|---|---|---|
| **CRUST** | 1½ cups vanilla wafer crumbs | ¼ cup finely chopped pecans |
| | ¼ cup granulated sugar | 6 tablespoons ( ¾ stick) sweet butter, softened |
| **FILLING** | 1½ pounds creamed cottage cheese | 1 teaspoon vanilla extract |
| | ½ cup granulated sugar | ½ cup light cream |
| | 2 eggs | 2 cups canned peaches, drained and crushed |
| **TOPPING** | 1½ cups sour cream | 1 cup canned sliced peaches, drained |
| | 1 tablespoon granulated sugar | |
| **PAN** | 9-inch springform pan | |

CRUST   In a medium-size bowl, combine the vanilla wafer crumbs, sugar, chopped pecans, and butter. Blend well with fingers, fork, or pastry blender. Press or pat the mixture onto the bottom and sides of a well-buttered springform pan. Chill in the freezer or refrigerator for 15 minutes.

FILLING   In a large bowl, beat the cottage cheese, sugar, and eggs until smooth. Add the vanilla and light cream and continue to beat until smooth and fairly thick. Gently fold in the crushed peaches. Pour the mixture into the chilled pan. Place the spring-form pan inside of a larger pan containing 1 inch of water and bake in a preheated 325°F oven for 1½ hours. Transfer the cake to a wire rack and allow to cool for 30 minutes.

TOPPING   In a small mixing bowl, beat the sour cream and sugar until smooth. Spread the mixture evenly over the top of the cake and bake in a preheated 350° oven for 5 minutes. Transfer the cake to a wire rack and let cool completely. Remove the sides of the springform pan and decorate the top of the cake with the sliced peaches. Refrigerate overnight. Remove the cake from the refrigerator 2 hours before serving.

# ROQUEFORT AND PEACH
# CHEESECAKE

*For those who delight in the piquancy of one of the finest cheeses
in the world. Just the right amount of Roquefort, carefully
blended into the cream cheese mixture and topped with the
gentle sweetness of peaches, will please the most discriminating
cheese lover. You'll note that during baking the pungent
Roquefort aroma diminishes and the cake's flavor becomes
reminiscent of a quiche. This is an excellent choice for a wine
and cheese party or to serve as an appetizer.*

| | | |
|---|---|---|
| CRUST | 2½ cups graham cracker crumbs<br>½ cup granulated sugar | 6 tablespoons ( ¾ stick) sweet butter, softened |
| FILLING | 1½ pounds cream cheese, softened<br>½ cup granulated sugar<br>2 eggs | ½ cup sour cream<br>¼ teaspoon salt<br>6 ounces Roquefort cheese, softened |
| TOPPING | 1½ cups sour cream<br>2 tablespoons granulated sugar | 2½ cups canned sliced peaches, with syrup |
| PAN | 9-inch springform pan | |

CRUST  In a medium-size bowl, combine the graham cracker
crumbs, sugar, and butter. Blend well with fingers, fork, or pastry
blender. Press or pat the mixture onto the bottom and sides of a
well-buttered springform pan. Chill the pan in the freezer or
refrigerator for about 30 minutes.

FILLING  In a large bowl, beat the cream cheese and sugar until
very smooth. Add the eggs, sour cream, and salt and beat until
very smooth. Add the Roquefort cheese and beat again until very

smooth and creamy. Pour the mixture into the chilled pan. Place the springform pan inside of a larger pan containing 1 inch of water and bake in a preheated 325° oven for 1½ hours. Transfer the cake to a wire rack and let cool for 30 minutes. Note: The cake will not be set.

**TOPPING** In a small mixing bowl, combine the sour cream and 1 tablespoon of the sugar and beat until very smooth. Spread the mixture evenly over the top of the cake and bake in a preheated 350° oven for 5 minutes. Transfer the cake to a wire rack, letting it cool completely. Then chill in the refrigerator for 2 hours. When chilled, remove the sides of the springform pan and decorate the top of the cake with the sliced peaches. In a small skillet, combine about 3 ounces of the peach syrup and the remaining 1 tablespoon sugar and bring to a boil. Spread the glaze mixture over the peaches, then refrigerate overnight. For best results, remove the cake from the refrigerator at least 2 hours before serving.

# PINEAPPLE CHEESECAKE

*Plain pineapple cheesecake has long been an old favorite.*
*Add a sour cream topping and pineapple rings, and the cake*
*becomes a minor masterpiece.*

CRUST
2¼ cups graham cracker
    crumbs
¼ cup granulated sugar

6 tablespoons (¾ stick)
    sweet butter, softened
1 cup canned crushed
    pineapple, drained

FILLING
1 pound cream cheese,
    softened
½ pound creamed
    cottage cheese

½ cup granulated sugar
1 teaspoon vanilla extract
½ cup heavy cream
2 eggs

TOPPING
1½ cups sour cream
1 tablespoon granulated
    sugar

16 ounces canned
    pineapple rings,
    drained

PAN
9-inch springform pan

CRUST   In a medium-size bowl, combine the graham cracker crumbs, sugar, and butter. Blend well with fingers, fork, or pastry blender. Press or pat the mixture onto the bottom and sides of a well-buttered springform pan. Pour the crushed pineapple onto the bottom of the crust, then chill in the freezer or refrigerator for about 30 minutes.

FILLING   In a large bowl, beat the cream cheese, cottage cheese, and sugar until very smooth. Add the vanilla, heavy cream, and eggs and continue to beat until smooth. Pour the mixture into the chilled pan. Place the springform pan inside a larger pan containing 1 inch of water and bake in a preheated 325°F oven for 1½ hours. Transfer the cake to a wire rack and allow to cool for 30 minutes.

TOPPING   In a small mixing bowl, beat the sour cream and sugar until smooth, then spread the mixture evenly over the top of the cake and bake in a preheated 350° oven for 5 minutes. Transfer the cake to a wire rack and let cool completely. Remove the sides of the springform pan and decorate the top of the cake with the pineapple rings. Refrigerate overnight. Remove the cake from the refrigerator at least 2 hours before serving.

# HOLIDAY PUMPKIN CHEESECAKE

*An ideal choice for Halloween and Thanksgiving entertaining: a delicate gingersnap crust; a light and creamy filling flavored with pumpkin puree and spiced with nutmeg, ground cloves, and allspice; and a topping of whipped cream and chopped pecans.*

| | | |
|---|---|---|
| CRUST | ½ cup gingersnap crumbs | |
| FILLING | 2 pounds cream cheese, softened | 1 teaspoon grated nutmeg |
| | 1½ cups granulated sugar | 1 teaspoon ground cloves |
| | ⅓ cup all-purpose flour, sifted | ¼ teaspoon allspice |
| | 1½ teaspoons ground cinnamon | ⅛ teaspoon salt |
| | | 6 eggs |
| | | 2 cups pumpkin puree |
| TOPPING | 1 cup heavy cream | ½ cup chopped pecans |
| PAN | 9-inch springform pan | |

CRUST   Sprinkle the gingersnap crumbs onto the bottom and sides of a well-buttered springform pan. Chill until ready for filling.

FILLING In a large bowl, beat the cream cheese, sugar, flour, cinnamon, nutmeg, cloves, allspice, salt, and eggs until smooth. Add the pumpkin puree and continue to beat until very smooth. Pour the mixture into the chilled springform pan and bake in a preheated 325°F oven for 1½ hours. Turn off the oven and let the cake stand in the open oven for 30 minutes. Transfer to a wire rack and let cool completely.

TOPPING Carefully remove the sides of the springform pan. In a chilled bowl, whip the heavy cream and spread it over the top of the cake. Sprinkle the chopped pecans on top of the whipped cream. Transfer the cake to a serving dish and serve.

# RASPBERRY–ALMOND
# CHEESECAKE

*The simplicity of a jar of raspberry preserves can be effectively used to create a delicious dessert. A crunchy crust with chopped nuts, a hint of almond flavor in the filling, and a topping of raspberry preserves sprinkled with sliced almonds make a delightful dessert that is fast and easy to put together.*

| | | |
|---|---|---|
| CRUST | 1¾ cups graham cracker crumbs<br>½ cup finely chopped mixed nuts | ¼ cup granulated sugar<br>6 tablespoons (¾ stick) sweet butter, softened |
| FILLING | 1½ pounds cream cheese, softened<br>¾ cup granulated sugar<br>3 eggs | ½ cup heavy cream<br>⅛ teaspoon salt<br>1 teaspoon almond extract |
| TOPPING | 1 cup raspberry preserves | 1 cup finely sliced almonds |
| PAN | 9-inch springform pan | |

CRUST  In a medium-size bowl, combine the graham cracker crumbs, chopped mixed nuts, sugar, and butter. Blend well with fingers, fork, or pastry blender. Press or pat the mixture onto the bottom and sides of a well-buttered springform pan. Chill in the freezer or refrigerator for about 30 minutes.

FILLING  In a large bowl, beat the cream cheese, sugar, eggs, heavy cream, salt, and almond extract until very smooth and creamy. Pour into the chilled pan. Place the springform pan inside of a larger pan containing 1 inch of water and bake in a preheated 325°F oven for 1½ hours. Transfer the cake to a wire rack and allow to cool for 2 hours.

TOPPING   Spread the raspberry preserves evenly over the top of the cake, then decorate with sliced almonds. Carefully remove the sides of the springform pan and transfer the cake to a serving dish. Refrigerate for at least 2 hours before serving.

---

# OLD-FASHIONED STRAWBERRY CHEESECAKE

*This fresh-strawberry cheesecake could be considered a cousin to the traditional strawberry shortcake. The lightness of this unusual pie shell is due to the addition of heavy cream and an egg. The fresh strawberries in the filling and topping will stir the appetite, while its beauty and aroma draw compliments.*

SHELL
2 cups all-purpose flour, sifted
½ teaspoon salt
2 tablespoons granulated sugar
1 teaspoon baking powder
10 tablespoons (1¼ sticks) sweet butter, chilled
6 tablespoons heavy cream, lightly beaten with 1 egg yolk

FILLING
1½ pounds cream cheese, softened
½ cup granulated sugar
3 eggs
1 cup heavy cream
1 teaspoon vanilla extract
1 cup sliced fresh strawberries

TOPPING
1 cup heavy cream, whipped
1 cup whole fresh strawberries

PAN
9-inch springform pan

SHELL   In a large bowl, combine the flour, salt, sugar, baking powder, butter, and heavy cream. Blend well with fingers, fork, or pastry blender. Form the dough into a ball, knead lightly with the heel of the hand against a smooth surface for about 15 seconds, then reform it into a ball. Wrap it in wax paper and chill in the refrigerator for 1 hour. When chilled, roll out the dough on a floured surface until $\frac{3}{16}$ inch thick. Fit the dough into the springform pan, pressing it 2 inches up the sides of the pan and crimping the edge decoratively. Chill in the refrigerator or freezer for 30 minutes. Next, line the shell with wax paper, fill it with uncooked rice or dried beans, and bake it in a preheated 400°F oven for 8 minutes. Remove the rice and wax paper, prick the bottom of the shell all over with a fork, and return the shell to the oven for another 8 to 10 minutes. Transfer to a wire rack and allow to cool for 30 minutes.

FILLING   In a large bowl, beat the cream cheese, sugar, and eggs until very smooth. Add the heavy cream and vanilla and continue to beat until smooth and creamy. Gently fold in the sliced strawberries. Pour the mixture into the chilled shell and bake in a preheated 350° oven for 1 hour. Transfer the cake to a wire rack and let cool completely.

TOPPING   Carefully remove the sides of the springform pan and spread the whipped cream over the top of the cake. Place the whole strawberries decoratively on top of the whipped cream. Transfer the cake to a serving dish and either serve immediately or refrigerate.

# CONTINENTAL STRAWBERRY CHEESECAKE

*A combination using fresh strawberries and strawberry preserves. The fresh berries are suspended in a creamy cheesecake batter topped with a layer of strawberry preserves and toasted almonds. An excellent choice when strawberries are in season.*

**CRUST**
2 cups graham cracker crumbs
¼ cup finely ground almonds
¼ cup granulated sugar
6 tablespoons (¾ stick) sweet butter, softened

**FILLING**
1½ pounds cream cheese, softened
¾ cup granulated sugar
3 eggs
½ cup heavy cream
1½ teaspoons vanilla extract
1 cup sliced fresh strawberries

**TOPPING**
1 cup strawberry preserves
1 cup finely sliced almonds, toasted

**PAN**
9-inch springform pan

**CRUST** In a medium-size bowl, combine the graham cracker crumbs, ground almonds, sugar, and butter. Blend well with fingers, fork, or pastry blender. Press or pat the mixture onto the bottom and sides of a well-buttered springform pan. Chill in the freezer or refrigerator for about 30 minutes.

**FILLING** In a large bowl, beat the cream cheese, sugar, and eggs until very smooth. Add the heavy cream and vanilla, and continue to beat until very smooth and creamy. Fold in the sliced strawberries. Pour the mixture into the chilled pan. Place the springform pan inside of a larger pan containing 1 inch of water and bake in a preheated 325°F oven for 1½ hours. Transfer the cake to a wire rack and allow to cool completely.

TOPPING  Carefully remove the sides of the springform pan and spread the strawberry preserves evenly over the top of the cake. Then sprinkle the sliced almonds on top of the preserves. Transfer the cake to a serving dish and either serve immediately or refrigerate.

---

# STRAWBERRY CUSTARD CHEESECAKE

*This simple, easy cheesecake's very light and custardy filling and prepared strawberry topping make this a time-saving delight.*

| | | |
|---|---|---|
| CRUST | 1 cup graham cracker crumbs | 3 tablespoons sweet butter, softened |
| | 2 tablespoons granulated sugar | |
| FILLING | 1 pound cream cheese, softened | 1 cup heavy cream |
| | 4 eggs | 1 cup sour cream |
| | 2 teaspoons vanilla extract | 2 cups milk |
| | | ¾ cup granulated sugar |
| TOPPING | 21 ounces canned strawberry pie filling and topping | |
| PAN | 9-inch springform pan | |

CRUST  In a small mixing bowl, combine the graham cracker crumbs, sugar, and butter. Blend well with fingers, fork, or pastry blender. Press or pat the mixture onto the bottom of a well-buttered springform pan and chill in the freezer or refrigerator for 15 minutes.

FILLING In a large bowl, beat the cream cheese, eggs, vanilla, and heavy cream until smooth. Add the sour cream, milk, and sugar and continue to beat until very smooth and creamy. Pour the mixture into the chilled pan and bake in a preheated 450°F oven for 40 minutes. Transfer the cake to a wire rack and allow it to cool for 1 hour.

TOPPING Spread the strawberry topping evenly over the top of the cake and bake in a preheated 375° oven for 15 minutes. Transfer to a wire rack and allow to cool completely. Place the cake in the refrigerator for at least 2 hours. Then remove the sides of the springform pan and refrigerate overnight. Remove the cake from the refrigerator at least 2 hours before serving.

# STRAWBERRY–AMARETTO
# CHEESECAKE

*A union of two popular flavors, this cheesecake consists of a graham cracker crust and a very creamy cream cheese filling flavored with lemon, brandy, and vanilla extract, to which roughly cut strawberries have been added. The remaining cut strawberries, which have been marinated in Amaretto and sugar, form the delectable topping.*

**CRUST**
1 cup graham cracker crumbs
¼ cup granulated sugar
2 tablespoons sweet butter, softened

**FILLING**
2 pounds cream cheese, softened
1½ cups granulated sugar
1 cup heavy cream
6 eggs
3 tablespoons lemon juice
½ teaspoon brandy extract
1 cup sour cream
1 tablespoon vanilla extract
2 tablespoons all-purpose flour, sifted
1 cup chopped fresh strawberries

**TOPPING**
2½ cups chopped fresh strawberries
1 cup Amaretto liqueur
1 tablespoon granulated sugar

**PAN**
9-inch springform pan

**CRUST** In a small mixing bowl, combine the graham cracker crumbs, sugar, and butter. Blend well with fingers, fork, or pastry blender. Press or pat the mixture onto the bottom of a well-buttered springform pan. Chill in the freezer or refrigerator for about 30 minutes.

FILLING In a large bowl, beat the cream cheese, sugar, and heavy cream until smooth. Add the eggs, one at a time, making sure that the mixture is smooth after beating in each egg. Add the lemon juice, brandy extract, sour cream, vanilla, and flour and continue to beat until very smooth and creamy. Fold in the chopped strawberries. Pour the mixture into the chilled spring-form pan and bake in a preheated 425°F oven for 15 minutes, then reduce the temperature to 275° and continue to bake for 1 hour. Transfer to a wire rack and allow to cool for 3 hours.

TOPPING In a medium-size bowl, marinate the strawberries in the Amaretto and sugar for about 3 to 4 hours. Spread the pre-pared strawberries evenly over the top of the cake and bake in a preheated 350° oven for 7 minutes. Transfer to a wire rack and allow to cool completely for about 2 hours. Remove the sides of the springform pan and refrigerate overnight. Remove the cake from the refrigerator at least 2 hours before serving.

# TROPICAL FRUIT
# CHEESECAKE

*A touch of paradise—the flavor of pineapple, coconut, and
mandarin oranges blend with the cream cheese and sour cream
to create an excitingly unique cheesecake. Black grapes and
bright orange slices decorate the topping of golden sour cream,
which is flavored with coconut, to yield a naturally colorful,
festive cake.*

**CRUST**
- 2¼ cups graham cracker crumbs
- 2 tablespoons granulated sugar
- 6 tablespoons (¾ stick) sweet butter, softened
- 1 cup canned crushed pineapple, drained

**FILLING**
- 1½ pounds cream cheese, softened
- ½ cup granulated sugar
- 2 eggs
- 1 teaspoon vanilla extract
- ¼ cup heavy cream
- ¼ cup milk

**TOPPING**
- 1½ cups sour cream
- 1 tablespoon granulated sugar
- 1 cup shredded coconut
- 2 drops yellow food coloring
- ½ cup fresh black grapes
- 1 cup canned mandarin orange slices, drained

**PAN**     9-inch springform pan

**CRUST** In a medium-size bowl, combine the graham cracker crumbs, sugar, and butter. Blend well with fingers, fork, or pastry blender. Press or pat the mixture onto the bottom and sides of a well-buttered springform pan. Pour the crushed pineapple onto the bottom of the crust, then chill in the freezer or refrigerator for 30 minutes.

FILLING  In a large bowl, beat the cream cheese, sugar, and eggs until very smooth. Add the vanilla, heavy cream, and milk and continue to beat until very smooth and creamy. Pour the mixture into the chilled pan. Place the springform pan inside of a larger pan containing 1 inch of water and bake in a preheated 325°F oven for 1½ hours. Transfer the cake to a wire rack and allow to cool for 30 minutes.

TOPPING  In a small mixing bowl, beat the sour cream, sugar, coconut, and yellow food coloring until smooth. Spread the mixture evenly over the top of the cake and bake in a preheated 375° oven for 5 minutes. Transfer the cake to a wire rack and let cool completely for 2 to 3 hours. Remove the sides of the springform pan and decorate the top of the cake with the black grapes and mandarin orange slices. Refrigerate overnight. Remove from the refrigerator at least 2 hours before serving.

# Cheesecakes
# with
# Nuts

## ALMOND PASTRY
## CHEESECAKE

*It is the precise amount of almond extract that makes this
cheesecake unique. Each slice of this gourmet cheesecake
will be savored as a delicate piece of pastry.*

CRUST
1 cup vanilla wafer
  crumbs
½ cup finely chopped
  almonds
¼ cup granulated sugar
4 tablespoons ( ½ stick)
  sweet butter, softened

FILLING
1½ pounds cream cheese,
  softened
¾ cup granulated sugar
2 eggs
½ cup light cream
1½ teaspoons almond
  extract
1½ teaspoons powdered
  sugar

PAN
9-inch springform pan

CRUST  In a small mixing bowl, combine the vanilla wafer
crumbs, chopped almonds, sugar, and butter. Blend well with
fingers, fork, or pastry blender. Press or pat mixture onto the
bottom of a well-buttered springform pan. Chill in the freezer
or refrigerator for about 30 minutes.

FILLING  In a large bowl, beat the cream cheese and sugar until smooth. Slowly mix in the eggs. Add the light cream and almond extract and beat until smooth. Pour the mixture into the chilled pan. Place the springform pan inside of a larger pan containing 1 inch of water and bake in a preheated 325°F oven for 1½ hours. Transfer the cake to a wire rack, letting it cool completely. Remove the sides of the springform pan and refrigerate at least 2 hours. Sprinkle the top of the cake with the powdered sugar before serving.

———

# ALMOND AND PINE NUT
# CHEESECAKE

*A jewel of a cake—light, creamy, and reminiscent of fine Italian pastry. The delicate blend of almond paste with the unique taste of the pine nuts entitles this cake to be dubbed a "crown prince" among cheesecakes.*

| | | |
|---|---|---|
| SHELL | 1½ cups all-purpose flour, sifted | ¼ pound (1 stick) sweet butter, softened |
| | ¼ cup granulated sugar | 1 egg |
| FILLING | 1 cup apricot preserve | 1 teaspoon Amaretto liqueur |
| | 1½ pounds cream cheese, softened | 2 ounces almond paste |
| | ½ cup granulated sugar | ½ cup pine nuts |
| | 2 eggs | 1½ teaspoons powdered sugar |
| | 1 teaspoon almond extract | |
| PAN | 9-inch springform pan | |

SHELL  In a large bowl, combine the flour, sugar, butter, and egg. Blend well with fingers, fork, or pastry blender. Form the dough into a ball, knead lightly with the heel of the hand against a smooth surface for a few seconds, then reform it into a ball. Wrap it in wax paper and chill in the refrigerator for 1 hour. When chilled, roll out the dough on a floured surface until ⅛ inch thick. Fit the dough into the springform pan, pressing it 2 inches up the sides of the pan and crimping the edge decoratively. Prick the bottom of the shell with a fork and chill in the freezer or refrigerator for 30 minutes. Next, line the shell with wax paper, fill it with uncooked rice or dried beans, and bake it in a preheated 350°F oven for 10 minutes. Carefully remove the rice and wax paper and bake the shell for another 10 minutes. Transfer the pan to a wire rack and allow to cool for 30 minutes. Spread the apricot preserve on the bottom of the cooled shell and chill in the refrigerator for 30 minutes.

FILLING   In a large bowl, beat the cream cheese, sugar, and eggs until very smooth. Add the almond extract, Amaretto, and almond paste and continue to beat until smooth. Pour the mixture into the chilled pan and sprinkle the pine nuts on top of it. Place the cake in a preheated 325° oven and bake for 1½ hours. Transfer to a wire rack and let cool completely. Carefully remove the sides of the springform pan and transfer the cake to a serving dish. Sprinkle the top of the cake with the powdered sugar and serve.

# ALMOND-AMARETTO
# CHEESECAKE

*The fragrance of almonds will fill the air with the promise of something very special. A dusting of graham cracker crumbs is used as the crust for a very moist and creamy filling, which is flavored with Amaretto liqueur, orange juice, and vanilla extract, and topped with a sprinkling of finely chopped almonds.*

CAKE

½ cup graham cracker crumbs
2½ pounds cream cheese, softened
¾ cup granulated sugar
5 eggs

¼ cup Amaretto liqueur
1 tablespoon orange juice
1 teaspoon vanilla extract
2 tablespoons finely chopped blanched almonds

PAN    10-inch springform pan

Sprinkle the graham cracker crumbs onto the bottom and sides of a well-buttered springform pan. Pour out the excess crumbs. In a large bowl, beat the cream cheese and sugar until smooth. Add the eggs, one at a time, beating the mixture well after each addition. Blend in the Amaretto, orange juice, and vanilla and continue to beat until very smooth and creamy. Pour the mixture into the coated pan. Place the springform pan inside of a larger pan containing 1 inch of water and bake in a preheated 350°F oven for 1¾ hours. Turn off the oven and let the cake stand in the closed oven for 30 minutes. Transfer to a wire rack and allow to cool to room temperature. Remove the sides of the springform pan and sprinkle the top of the cake with the chopped almonds. Refrigerate overnight. Remove the cake from the refrigerator 2 hours before serving.

# CASHEW AND PECAN
# CHEESECAKE

*This good-looking and delicious nut cake boasts a delicate crust
of butter cookies and chopped cashews, and a creamy filling
specked with finely chopped pecans and cashews and topped
with whipped cream and a sprinkling of more nuts. Looks
like an ice cream parlor concoction, but your guests will be
pleasantly surprised by the lightness of this cake.*

**CRUST**

1¼ cups butter cookie crumbs

¼ cup granulated sugar

¼ cup finely chopped cashews

3 tablespoons sweet butter, softened

**FILLING**

1½ pounds cream cheese, softened

1 cup light brown sugar

3 eggs

1 teaspoon vanilla extract

½ cup milk

½ cup chopped pecans

½ cup chopped cashews

**TOPPING**

1 cup heavy cream, whipped

¼ cup finely chopped cashews

½ cup whole pecans

**PAN**　　9-inch springform pan

**CRUST** In a small mixing bowl, combine the butter cookie crumbs, sugar, cashews, and butter. Blend well with fingers, fork, or pastry blender. Press or pat the mixture onto the bottom and sides of a well-buttered springform pan. Chill in the freezer or refrigerator for about 30 minutes.

**FILLING** In a large bowl, beat the cream cheese, sugar, eggs, vanilla, and milk until very smooth. Fold in the chopped nuts. Pour the mixture into the chilled pan. Place the springform pan inside of a larger pan containing 1 inch of water and bake in a preheated 325°F oven for 1½ hours. Transfer the cake to a wire rack and allow to cool for 3 hours.

**TOPPING** Carefully remove the sides of the springform pan and spread the whipped cream over the top of the cake. Decorate by sprinkling the chopped cashews and whole pecans on top of the whipped cream. Transfer the cake to a serving dish and serve.

---

# COCONUT CHEESECAKE

*Coconut, the fruit of tropical lands, rewards us with an almost indescribably delicious dessert. The uniting of coconut extract with cottage cheese, heavy cream, and sour cream, along with sugar and eggs, creates a creamy coconut-custard-type cheesecake. Topped with shredded coconut, this will delight the eye as much as the palate.*

| | | |
|---|---|---|
| **CRUST** | 2 cups Social Tea cracker crumbs | 4 tablespoons ( ½ stick) sweet butter, softened |
| **FILLING** | 1½ pounds creamed cottage cheese<br>1 cup granulated sugar<br>1½ teaspoons coconut extract | 4 eggs<br>1 cup sour cream<br>1 cup heavy cream |
| **TOPPING** | 1½ cups sour cream<br>1 tablespoon granulated sugar | ¼ cup shredded coconut<br>1 maraschino cherry |
| **PAN** | 10-inch springform pan | |

**CRUST** In a medium-size bowl, combine the social tea cracker crumbs and butter. Blend well with fingers, fork, or pastry blender. Press or pat the mixture onto the bottom and sides of a well-buttered springform pan. Chill in the freezer or refrigerator for 30 minutes.

**FILLING**    In a large bowl, beat the cottage cheese, sugar, coconut extract, and 1 egg until smooth. Then add the remaining 3 eggs, one at a time, and beat until very smooth. Add the sour cream and heavy cream and continue to beat until very creamy and smooth. Pour the mixture into the chilled pan. Place the springform pan inside of a larger pan containing 1 inch of water and bake in a preheated 350°F oven for 1¼ hours. Transfer the cake to a wire rack and allow to cool for 30 minutes.

**TOPPING**    In a small mixing bowl, combine the sour cream, sugar, and shredded coconut and beat until smooth. Spread the mixture evenly over the top of the cake and bake in a preheated 350° oven for 5 minutes. Transfer to a wire rack and let cool completely. Remove the sides of the springform pan and decorate the top of the cake with a cherry. Refrigerate overnight. Remove the cake from the refrigerator at least 2 hours before serving.

# MACADAMIA–MOCHA CHEESECAKE

*Hawaii sends her aloha with this unusual approach to enjoying the delicious macadamia. The combination of macadamia nuts with cream cheese, which has been flavored with a mocha of pure cocoa and instant coffee, will delight the most discerning dessert lovers.*

**CRUST**
1½ cups chocolate wafer crumbs
1 cup finely ground macadamia nuts
½ teaspoon ground cinnamon
¼ pound (1 stick) sweet butter, softened

**FILLING**
1 cup granulated sugar
3 eggs
1½ pounds cream cheese, softened
8 ounces semisweet baking chocolate
1 teaspoon instant coffee, dissolved in 1 teaspoon hot water
2 tablespoons unsweetened cocoa
1 teaspoon vanilla extract
3 cups sour cream
¾ cup chopped macadamia nuts
4 tablespoons (½ stick) sweet butter, melted

**TOPPING**
1 cup heavy cream, whipped
1 ounce semisweet baking chocolate, to make 6
chocolate curls, each 2 inches long
½ cup whole macadamia nuts

**PAN**
10-inch springform pan

**CRUST** In a medium-size bowl, combine the chocolate wafer crumbs, ground macadamia nuts, cinnamon, and butter. Blend well with fingers, fork, or pastry blender. Press or pat the mixture onto the bottom and sides of a well-buttered springform pan. Chill in the freezer or refrigerator for 30 minutes.

FILLING   In a large bowl, beat the sugar and eggs until light and smooth, then beat in the cream cheese. Melt the chocolate in a double boiler and add to the mixture. Add the dissolved instant coffee, the cocoa, and the vanilla and continue to beat until very smooth. Beat in the sour cream and chopped macadamia nuts. Mix in the butter, then pour the mixture into the chilled spring-form pan and bake in a preheated 350°F oven for 45 minutes. Transfer to a wire rack to cool, then chill in the refrigerator for 2 hours.

TOPPING   Prepare chocolate curls by melting the chocolate, then spreading it thinly on a sheet of wax paper, and refrigerating it for 30 minutes. Then, with a flat knife scrape the chilled chocolate into long curls and cut them into 2-inch lengths.

When almost ready to serve, remove the sides of the spring-form pan, then decorate the top of the cake with whipped cream, chocolate curls, and whole macadamia nuts.

# SOUTHERN PECAN
# CHEESECAKE

*The South can be justifiably proud of this cake. A pecan pie in cheesecake form, with a sour cream topping, whole pecans, and slices of mandarin orange. A taste treat for those who love pecan pie.*

**CRUST**
1⅔ cups graham cracker crumbs
½ cup finely chopped pecans

¼ pound (1 stick) sweet butter

**FILLING**
2 pounds cream cheese, softened
3 eggs
1 teaspoon vanilla extract

2 cups light brown sugar
1 cup finely chopped pecans
3 tablespoons flour

**TOPPING**
1½ cups sour cream
1 tablespoon granulated sugar
1 teaspoon vanilla extract

½ cup whole pecans
½ cup canned mandarin orange slices, drained

**PAN**
10-inch springform pan

**CRUST** In a medium-size bowl, combine the graham cracker crumbs, chopped pecans, and butter. Blend well with fingers, fork, or pastry blender. Pat or press the mixture onto the bottom and sides of a well-buttered springform pan. Chill in the freezer or refrigerator for 30 minutes.

**FILLING** In a large bowl, beat the cream cheese, eggs, and vanilla until very smooth. Add the sugar, pecans, and flour and beat until smooth and creamy. Pour the mixture into the chilled pan and bake in a preheated 350°F oven for 1 hour and 10 minutes. Transfer the cake to a wire rack and allow to cool for about 30 minutes.

**TOPPING**    In a small mixing bowl, combine the sour cream, sugar, and vanilla and beat until smooth. Spread the mixture evenly over the top of the cake and bake in a preheated 375° oven for 5 minutes. Transfer the cake to a wire rack and let cool completely. Carefully remove the sides of the springform pan and decorate the top of the cake with the whole pecans and mandarin orange slices. Refrigerate overnight. Remove the cake from the refrigerator 2 hours before serving.

———

# PRUNE AND PECAN
# CHEESECAKE

*Sharing a nodding acquaintance with the prune danish,*
*this cheesecake's light, creamy filling combines cooked prunes*
*and finely chopped pecans, and is topped with sour cream and*
*whole pecans. A delightful change for any cheesecake enthusiast.*

CRUST
2 cups graham cracker
crumbs
¼ cup finely ground
pecans

¼ cup granulated sugar
6 tablespoons (¾ stick)
sweet butter, softened

FILLING
1½ pounds creamed
cottage cheese
½ cup granulated sugar
2 eggs
½ cup sour cream
½ cup heavy cream
½ teaspoon vanilla
extract

1 teaspoon ground
cinnamon
½ teaspoon allspice
1 cup prunes, cooked,
drained, pitted, and
chopped
1 cup finely chopped
pecans

TOPPING
1½ cups sour cream
2 tablespoons granulated
sugar

½ cup whole pecans

PAN
9-inch springform pan

CRUST In a medium-size bowl, combine the graham cracker crumbs, ground pecans, sugar, and butter. Blend well with fingers, fork, or pastry blender. Press or pat the mixture onto the bottom and sides of a well-buttered springform pan. Chill in the freezer or refrigerator for about 30 minutes.

FILLING In a large bowl, beat the cottage cheese, sugar, and eggs until very smooth. Add the sour cream, heavy cream, and vanilla, and beat until smooth. Add the cinnamon and allspice and mix well. Add the chopped prunes and pecans and mix well. Pour the mixture into the chilled pan. Place the springform pan inside of a larger pan containing 1 inch of water and bake in a preheated 325°F oven for 1½ hours. Transfer to a wire rack and allow to cool for 30 minutes.

TOPPING    In a small mixing bowl, beat the sour cream and sugar until smooth. Spread the mixture evenly over the top of the cake and bake in a preheated 350° oven for 5 minutes. Transfer to a wire rack and allow to cool completely. Carefully remove the sides of the springform pan and decorate the top of the cake with whole pecans. Transfer to a serving dish and serve.

# COUNTRY PRALINE CHEESECAKE

*Reminiscent of the crisp, caramel confections for which it's named, this cheesecake uses a graham cracker crust, an extra creamy cream cheese filling, and a topping of whipped cream and ground pecan praline.*

**CRUST**
1 cup graham cracker crumbs
3 tablespoons granulated sugar
3 tablespoons sweet butter, softened

**FILLING**
1½ pounds cream cheese, softened
6 egg yolks
1 tablespoon lemon juice
1 teaspoon vanilla extract
1 cup heavy cream
2 egg whites
⅛ teaspoon cream of tartar
⅛ teaspoon salt

**TOPPING**
¾ cup granulated sugar
¼ cup water
⅛ teaspoon cream of tartar
½ cup chopped pecans
1 cup heavy cream, whipped

**PAN**
9-inch springform pan

**CRUST** In a small mixing bowl, combine the graham cracker crumbs, sugar, and butter. Blend well with fingers, fork, or pastry blender. Press or pat the mixture onto the bottom of a well-buttered springform pan. Chill in the freezer or refrigerator for approximately 30 minutes.

**FILLING** In a large bowl, beat the cream cheese until light and creamy. Add the egg yolks, one at a time, beating well after each addition. Stir in the lemon juice and vanilla. In a separate, chilled small mixing bowl, beat the heavy cream until it holds stiff peaks. In another medium-size bowl, beat the egg whites with the cream of tartar and salt until the whites hold their peaks. Fold the whipped cream and egg whites into the cheese mixture and pour the entire mixture into the chilled pan. Bake in a preheated 300°F oven for 1 hour, then reduce the temperature to 250° and bake for another hour. Open the oven door and let the cake sit in the open oven until completely cooled. Chill in the refrigerator for 3 hours. Carefully remove the sides of the springform pan and transfer the cake to a serving dish.

**TOPPING**　In a skillet, combine the sugar, water, and cream of tartar. Over medium heat, bring the mixture to a boil and continue cooking for 3 minutes, stirring, until it forms a syrup that is a light caramel color. Add the chopped pecans and swirl them around in the skillet until the nuts are fully coated. Pour the mixture into a lightly oiled pan and let cool until hard. On a wooden chopping board, chop the finished praline into coarse bits. Then pulverize the chopped praline using a wooden bowl and pestle or a rolling pin and wax paper. Decorate the top of the cake with the whipped cream and sprinkle the praline over the cream. Either serve immediately or refrigerate.

# HONEY-WALNUT
# CHEESECAKE

*A crunchy crust of honey graham crackers and ground walnuts supports the creamy, light mixture of cheese, honey, and chopped walnuts. The topping is sour cream with finely ground walnuts. Carefully baked at a low temperature, this is an appealing dessert treat.*

**CRUST**
2 cups honey graham cracker crumbs
½ cup finely ground walnuts

6 tablespoons (¾ stick) sweet butter, softened

**FILLING**
1½ pounds cream cheese, softened
½ cup honey
3 eggs

½ teaspoon vanilla extract
1 cup heavy cream
¾ cup chopped walnuts

**TOPPING**
1½ cups sour cream
¼ cup granulated sugar

½ cup finely ground walnuts

**PAN**
9-inch springform pan

**CRUST** In a medium-size bowl, combine the honey graham cracker crumbs, walnuts, and butter. Blend well with fingers, fork, or pastry blender. Press or pat the mixture onto the bottom and sides of a well-buttered springform pan. Chill in the freezer or refrigerator for about 30 minutes.

**FILLING** In a large bowl, beat the cream cheese, honey, and eggs until very smooth. Add the vanilla and heavy cream and continue to beat until very smooth. Fold in the chopped walnuts. Pour the mixture into the chilled pan. Place the springform pan inside of a larger pan containing 1 inch of water and bake in a preheated 325°F oven for 1½ hours. Transfer the cake to a wire rack and allow to cool for about 30 minutes.

TOPPING   In a small mixing bowl, beat the sour cream and sugar until smooth. Spread the mixture evenly over the top of the cake and bake in a preheated 350° oven for 5 minutes. Transfer to a wire rack and let cool completely. Carefully remove the sides of the springform pan and decorate the top of the cake with ground walnuts. Transfer to a serving dish and either serve immediately or refrigerate.

# MAPLE–WALNUT CHEESECAKE

*This cheesecake, which may well be served à la mode, consists of a crunchy crust of vanilla wafers and chopped walnuts; a maple-flavored, light and creamy filling; and a topping mixture of sour cream, maple syrup, and sugar, with a sprinkle of chopped walnuts. Why waste your maple syrup on pancakes and waffles?*

**CRUST**
1¾ cups vanilla wafer crumbs
½ cup finely chopped walnuts

¼ cup granulated sugar
6 tablespoons (¾ stick) sweet butter, softened

**FILLING**
1½ pounds cream cheese, softened
½ cup granulated sugar
2 eggs
¼ teaspoon salt

1 teaspoon maple flavoring
¼ cup heavy cream
½ cup milk

**TOPPING**
1½ cups sour cream
1 tablespoon granulated sugar

2 teaspoons maple syrup
1 cup finely chopped walnuts

**PAN**
9-inch springform pan

**CRUST** In a medium-size bowl, combine the vanilla wafer crumbs, chopped walnuts, sugar, and butter. Blend well with fingers, fork, or pastry blender. Press or pat the mixture onto the bottom and sides of a well-buttered springform pan. Chill in the freezer or refrigerator for about 30 minutes.

**FILLING** In a large bowl, beat the cream cheese, sugar, eggs, and salt until smooth. Add the maple flavoring, heavy cream, and milk and continue to beat until very smooth and creamy. Pour the mixture into the chilled pan. Place the springform pan inside of a larger pan containing 1 inch of water and bake in a preheated 325°F oven for 1½ hours. Transfer the cake to a wire rack and allow to cool for 30 minutes.

TOPPING   In a small mixing bowl, beat the sour cream, sugar, and maple syrup until very smooth. Spread the mixture evenly over the top of the cake and bake in a preheated 350° oven for 5 minutes. Transfer to a wire rack and allow to cool completely. Remove the sides of the springform pan and sprinkle the chopped walnuts all over the top of the cake. Refrigerate overnight. Remove the cake from the refrigerator at least 2 hours before serving.

# WALNUT–PEACH
# CHEESECAKE

*Walnuts and peaches go well together. In this recipe finely
ground walnuts are in the crust, while peach preserve,
bite-size bits of peach, and chopped walnuts enhance the filling.
The topping of sliced peaches and ground walnuts is the
finishing touch to this very attractive and appetizing cheesecake.
Serve as is or à la mode with vanilla ice cream.*

**CRUST**  2 cups graham cracker crumbs
½ cup finely ground walnuts
¼ cup granulated sugar
6 tablespoons ( ¾ stick) sweet butter, softened

**FILLING**  1 cup peach preserve
1½ pounds cream cheese, softened
½ cup granulated sugar
2 eggs
1 teaspoon vanilla extract
1 teaspoon peach liqueur
½ cup canned peaches, drained and chopped
½ cup finely chopped walnuts

**TOPPING**  1½ cups sour cream
¼ cup granulated sugar
1 cup canned sliced peaches, drained
¼ cup finely ground walnuts

**PAN**  9-inch springform pan

**CRUST**  In a medium-size bowl, combine the graham cracker
crumbs, walnuts, sugar, and butter. Blend well with fingers, fork,
or pastry blender. Press or pat the mixture onto the bottom and
sides of a well-buttered springform pan. Spread the peach preserve on the bottom of the crust and chill in the freezer or refrigerator for about 30 minutes.

FILLING In a large bowl, beat the cream cheese, sugar, and eggs until very smooth. Add the vanilla and peach liqueur and beat well until smooth. Add the chopped peaches and walnuts and mix well. Pour the mixture into the chilled pan and refrigerate for 1 hour. Place the springform pan inside of a larger pan containing 1 inch of water and bake in a preheated 325°F oven for 1½ hours. Transfer the cake to a wire rack and allow to cool for 30 minutes.

TOPPING In a small mixing bowl, beat the sour cream and sugar until smooth. Spread the mixture evenly over the top of the cake and bake in a preheated 350° oven for 5 minutes. Transfer to a wire rack and let cool completely. Carefully remove the sides of the springform pan and decorate the top of the cake with the sliced peaches. Sprinkle the ground walnuts on top of the sliced peaches. Transfer the cake to a serving dish and either serve immediately or refrigerate.

# MIXED NUT CHEESECAKE

*A mingling of selected nuts, for those who enjoy a variety of tastes and aromas. The nuts are mixed with almond paste and blended into the crust mixture while the almond extract flavors the cream cheese batter. This cake will please the palate of those who are nuts about nuts!*

**CRUST**
2¼ cups graham cracker crumbs
¼ cup finely chopped mixed nuts (almonds, hazelnuts, peanuts, walnuts, and cashews)
¼ cup granulated sugar
1 teaspoon almond paste
6 tablespoons (¾ stick) sweet butter, softened

**FILLING**
1½ pounds cream cheese, softened
¾ cup granulated sugar
2 eggs
¼ cup heavy cream
¼ cup milk
¼ teaspoon salt
1½ teaspoons almond extract

**TOPPING**
1½ cups sour cream
1 tablespoon granulated sugar
1 teaspoon almond extract
¼ cup finely chopped mixed nuts

**PAN**
9-inch springform pan

**CRUST** In a medium-size bowl, combine the graham cracker crumbs, chopped mixed nuts, sugar, almond paste, and butter. Blend well with fingers, fork, or pastry blender. Press or pat the mixture onto the bottom and sides of a well-buttered springform pan. Chill in the freezer or refrigerator for 30 minutes.

**FILLING** In a large bowl, beat the cream cheese and sugar until very smooth. Beat in the eggs, one at a time. Add the heavy cream, milk, salt, and almond extract and beat until very smooth.

Pour the mixture into the chilled pan. Place the springform pan inside of a larger pan containing 1 inch of water and bake in a preheated 325°F oven for 1½ hours. Transfer the cake to a wire rack and let cool for 30 minutes. Note: The cake will not be set.

TOPPING   In a small mixing bowl, combine the sour cream, sugar, and almond extract. Beat until very smooth. Spread the mixture evenly over the top of the cake and bake in a preheated 350° oven for 5 minutes. Transfer the cake to a wire rack, letting it cool completely. Carefully remove the sides of the springform pan and sprinkle the outer edge of the cake with the chopped nuts. Refrigerate overnight. For best results, remove the cake from the refrigerator at least 2 hours before serving.

# Cheesecakes
# from Around
# the World

## CLASSIC EUROPEAN
## CHEESECAKE

*There are many variations of this classic; this one is a*
*basic recipe, easy to prepare, light, creamy, and delectable.*
*Serve it with coffee for a grand finale to a fine dinner.*

**CAKE**

1 pound cream cheese, softened
1 pound ricotta cheese
1½ cups granulated sugar
4 large eggs
4 tablespoons (½ stick) sweet butter, melted

3 tablespoons all-purpose flour, sifted
3 tablespoons cornstarch
2½ teaspoons vanilla extract
2 cups sour cream
1½ teaspoons powdered sugar

**PAN**  9-inch springform pan

In a large bowl, beat the cream cheese, ricotta cheese, sugar, and eggs until very smooth. Add the melted butter, flour, cornstarch, and vanilla and continue to beat until smooth. Fold in the sour cream. Pour the mixture into an ungreased springform pan and bake in a preheated 325°F oven for 1 hour. When done, turn off the oven, but do not open the oven door; let the cake cool in the closed oven for 2 hours. Transfer to a wire rack and

allow to cool for 2 hours more. Remove the sides of the springform pan and decorate the top of the cake with the powdered
sugar. Refrigerate for 2 hours before serving.

———————

# EUROPEAN PINEAPPLE
# CHEESECAKE

*Great to have on hand in the freezer. This cheesecake blends
a crunchy crust of graham crackers and chopped walnuts; a light,
textured, pot cheese filling with crushed pineapple; and a
topping of fresh whipped cream and chopped walnuts.
All but the topping can be prepared ahead of time and frozen
and, when ready to use, thawed to room temperature and
topped with the whipped cream and walnuts.*

| | | |
|---|---|---|
| CRUST | 2 cups graham cracker crumbs | ¼ cup granulated sugar |
| | ¼ cup finely chopped walnuts | 6 tablespoons (¾ stick) sweet butter, softened |
| FILLING | 2 pounds pot cheese | 2 tablespoons cornstarch |
| | 4 tablespoons (½ stick) sweet butter, melted | 1 cup heavy cream |
| | ½ cup granulated sugar | 1 cup canned crushed pineapple, drained |
| | 3 eggs, separated | |
| TOPPING | 1 cup heavy cream | ½ cup chopped walnuts |
| PAN | 10-inch springform pan | |

CRUST   In a medium-size bowl, combine the graham cracker
crumbs, walnuts, sugar, and butter. Blend well with fingers, fork,
or pastry blender. Press or pat the mixture onto the bottom and
sides of a well-buttered springform pan. Chill in the freezer or
refrigerator for 30 minutes.

FILLING   In a large bowl, beat the pot cheese, melted butter, sugar, and egg yolks until smooth. Add the cornstarch and heavy cream and continue to beat until very smooth. In a separate bowl, beat the egg whites until they hold their peaks. Add to the cheese mixture and fold in until smooth. Fold in the crushed pineapple. Pour the mixture into the chilled springform pan and bake in a preheated 350°F oven for 1 hour. Transfer the cake to a wire rack and allow to cool completely.

TOPPING   In a chilled small mixing bowl, whip the heavy cream and spread it evenly over the top of the cake. Sprinkle the chopped walnuts on top of the cream. Carefully remove the sides of the springform pan and transfer the cake to a serving dish. Refrigerate overnight for best results. Remove from the refrigerator 2 hours before serving. (You may wait to prepare this topping until just before serving if you prefer that the whipped cream be absolutely fresh and at its most luscious.)

# OLD-COUNTRY CHEESECAKE

*A truly wonderful cheesecake, the classic recipe for which has been brought to us from several European countries. The delicate texture and low-fat content of the pot cheese or farmer cheese makes this cake extremely light and creamy, while maintaining a lower caloric value. This cake is best served at nearly room temperature.*

**CRUST**
2¼ cups vanilla wafer crumbs
1 cup granulated sugar

4 tablespoons (½ stick) sweet butter, melted
1 teaspoon ground cinnamon

**FILLING**
1 cup granulated sugar
4 eggs
⅛ teaspoon salt
1½ teaspoons vanilla extract
1 cup heavy cream

1½ pounds pot cheese or farmer cheese
¼ cup flour
½ teaspoon ground cinnamon

**PAN**
9-inch springform pan

**CRUST**   In a large bowl, combine the vanilla wafer crumbs, sugar, butter, and cinnamon. Blend well with fingers, fork, or pastry blender. Press or pat the mixture onto the bottom and sides of a well-buttered springform pan. Chill in the freezer or refrigerator for about 30 minutes.

**FILLING**   In a large bowl, beat the sugar and eggs until smooth, then add the salt, vanilla, and heavy cream. Beat well until the mixture is very smooth. Then add the pot cheese or farmer cheese and flour and beat until smooth. Press the mixture through a coarse sieve, then pour carefully into the chilled pan. Sprinkle the top of the cake with cinnamon and bake in a preheated 325°F oven for 1½ hours. Transfer the cake to a wire rack and let cool for about 3 hours. Carefully remove the sides of the springform pan and refrigerate overnight. Remove the cake from the refrigerator 2 hours before serving.

———————

# AUSTRIAN CHOCOLATE CHEESECAKE

*A great party cheesecake—lavish and delicious. The secret of this superb cake is the generous use of chocolate, chopped walnuts, and raspberry preserves.*

| | | |
|---|---|---|
| CRUST | 1¾ cups chocolate wafer crumbs<br>½ cup finely chopped walnuts | ½ cup granulated sugar<br>6 tablespoons (¾ stick) sweet butter, softened |
| FILLING | 1½ pounds cream cheese, softened<br>1 cup granulated sugar<br>3 eggs<br>½ cup heavy cream | 2 tablespoons sweet butter, melted<br>3½ tablespoons unsweetened cocoa<br>½ teaspoon chocolate flavoring |
| TOPPING | 1 cup raspberry preserve | ¾ cup chocolate sprinkles |
| PAN | 9-inch springform pan | |

CRUST  In a medium-size bowl, combine the chocolate wafer crumbs, walnuts, sugar, and butter. Blend well with fingers, fork, or pastry blender. Press or pat the mixture onto the bottom and sides of a well-buttered springform pan. Chill in the freezer or refrigerator for about 30 minutes.

FILLING  In a large bowl, beat the cream cheese, sugar, eggs, and heavy cream until very smooth and creamy. In a skillet, melt the butter and blend in the cocoa and chocolate flavoring, mixing until smooth. Add this to the cheese mixture and beat until very smooth. Pour into the chilled pan. Place the springform pan inside of a larger pan containing 1 inch of water and bake in a preheated 325°F oven for 1½ hours. Transfer the cake to a wire rack and allow to cool for at least 2 hours.

TOPPING  Spread the raspberry preserves evenly over the top of the cake. Gently sprinkle the chocolate sprinkles evenly on top of the raspberry preserves. Carefully remove the sides of the springform pan and transfer the cake to a serving dish. Refrigerate for 1 or 2 hours before serving.

---

# BAVARIAN CHOCOLATE CHEESECAKE

*This cheesecake has a distinctive taste. A light, bittersweet chocolate flavor, characteristic of the finest German pastries, predominates.*

CRUST
2¼ cups chocolate wafer crumbs
¼ cup granulated sugar
6 tablespoons ( ¾ stick) sweet butter, softened

FILLING
1½ pounds cream cheese, softened
¾ cup granulated sugar
2 eggs
½ cup light cream
¼ teaspoon salt
1½ ounces dark semisweet baking chocolate
2 teaspoons sweet butter

TOPPING
1½ cups sour cream
½ ounce dark semisweet baking chocolate
½ cup chocolate sprinkles
1 red maraschino cherry

PAN
9-inch springform pan

CRUST  In a medium-size bowl, combine chocolate wafer crumbs, sugar, and butter. Blend well with fingers, fork, or pastry blender. Press or pat the mixture onto the bottom and sides of a well-buttered springform pan. Chill in the freezer or refrigerator for about 30 minutes.

FILLING  In a large bowl, beat the cream cheese and sugar until smooth. Mix in the eggs, one at a time. Add the light cream and salt and continue to beat until smooth. In the top of a double boiler, melt the chocolate with the butter. Add the chocolate to the mixture and beat until very smooth and creamy. Pour into the chilled pan. Place the springform pan inside of a larger pan containing 1 inch of water and bake in a preheated 325°F oven for 1½ hours. Transfer the cake to a wire rack and allow to cool for 30 minutes. Note: The cake will not be set.

TOPPING  In a small mixing bowl, beat the sour cream and melted chocolate (melt chocolate in double boiler) until smooth. Spread the mixture evenly over the top of the cake and bake in a preheated 375° oven for 7 minutes. Transfer to a wire rack and allow to cool completely. Remove the sides of the pan and sprinkle the chocolate sprinkles on top of the cake. Place the cherry in the center. For best results, refrigerate the cake overnight but remove from the refrigerator at least 2 hours before serving.

# BOSTON CREAM
# CHEESECAKE

*This delightful cheesecake adapts to any occasion. It can be
served plain or topped with your favorite fruit. If the cake is not
fully set, it may crack, so be sure to allow it to cool
thoroughly before removing the sides of the springform pan.*

**CAKE**

1¼ pounds cream cheese, softened
1 cup granulated sugar
3 eggs
1 teaspoon vanilla extract
1 teaspoon almond extract
1 tablespoon lemon juice
3 cups sour cream
1½ teaspoons powdered sugar

**PAN**     9-inch springform pan

In a large bowl, beat the cream cheese and sugar until smooth.
Add the eggs, one at a time, beating until smooth. Add the
vanilla and almond extracts and the lemon juice and continue to
beat until smooth. Fold in the sour cream. Pour the mixture into
a well-buttered springform pan and bake in a preheated 350°F
oven for 45 minutes. Turn off the oven and let the cake stand in
the open oven for 1 hour. Transfer the cake to a wire rack and
allow to cool for 2 hours. Remove the sides of the springform pan
and refrigerate the cake overnight. Remove the cake from the
refrigerator 2 hours before serving and sprinkle the top with
the powdered sugar.

# CANADIAN CHEESECAKE

*Canada gives us this wonderful cake, particularly good for a large group. The gingersnap crust, the creamy filling and the topping of sour cream and chopped walnuts make it a treat for those who appreciate good cheesecake.*

| | | |
|---|---|---|
| **CRUST** | 1 cup gingersnap crumbs | 2 tablespoons sweet |
| | ¼ cup granulated sugar | butter, softened |
| **FILLING** | 1½ pounds cream cheese, | ⅛ cup all-purpose flour, |
| | softened | sifted |
| | 1 cup granulated sugar | 1 teaspoon lemon juice |
| | 4 eggs | 2 teaspoons vanilla extract |
| | 2 cups sour cream | 1 cup heavy cream |
| **TOPPING** | 1½ cups sour cream | ½ cup finely chopped |
| | 1 teaspoon vanilla extract | walnuts |
| | 2 tablespoons granulated | |
| | sugar | |
| **PAN** | 10-inch springform pan | |

**CRUST**  In a small mixing bowl, combine the gingersnap crumbs, sugar, and butter. Blend well with fingers, fork, or pastry blender. Press or pat the mixture onto the bottom of a well-buttered springform pan. Chill in the freezer or refrigerator for about 30 minutes.

**FILLING**  In a large bowl, beat the cream cheese, sugar, eggs, and sour cream until very smooth and creamy. Add the flour, lemon juice, vanilla, and heavy cream and continue to beat until smooth. Pour the mixture into the chilled pan and bake in a preheated 325°F oven for 15 minutes, then reduce the temperature to 300° and continue to bake for another 45 minutes. Turn off the oven and let the cake cool in the closed oven for 1 hour. Transfer to a wire rack and allow to cool for 30 minutes.

TOPPING  In a small mixing bowl, beat the sour cream, vanilla, and sugar until very smooth and creamy. Spread the mixture evenly over the top of the cake and bake in a preheated 350° oven for 5 minutes. Transfer to a wire rack and allow to cool completely. Carefully remove the sides of the springform pan and sprinkle the chopped walnuts on top of the cake. Refrigerate overnight. Remove from the refrigerator at least 2 hours before serving.

# DUTCH CHOCOLATE CHEESECAKE

*This simple-to-make, mellow cheesecake needs no embellishment and owes its popularity to the use of pure, unsweetened Dutch cocoa.*

CAKE
| | |
|---|---|
| 2 pounds cream cheese, softened | 3 tablespoons sweet butter |
| 1 cup granulated sugar | 6 tablespoons unsweet-ened Dutch cocoa |
| 3 eggs | |
| ½ cup heavy cream | 1 teaspoon vanilla extract |
| ½ cup sour cream | 1 teaspoon chocolate flavoring |

PAN  10-inch springform pan

In a large bowl, beat the cream cheese, sugar, and eggs until very smooth. Add the heavy cream and sour cream and continue to beat until very smooth and creamy. In a small skillet, melt the butter and mix in the cocoa until very smooth. Add to the cheese mixture and beat until extremely smooth. Add the vanilla and chocolate flavoring and mix well. Pour into a well-buttered springform pan. Place the springform pan inside of a larger pan containing 1 inch of water and bake in a preheated 325°F oven for 1½ hours. Transfer to a wire rack and allow to cool completely. Carefully remove the sides of the springform pan and transfer the cake to a serving dish. Refrigerate for at least 2 hours before serving. For best results, refrigerate overnight but remove from the refrigerator 2 hours before serving.

---

# PENN-DUTCH TRADITIONAL CHEESECAKE

*How simple can a cheesecake be? The pride of the Pennsylvania Dutch, this cake is simple and delicious, easy to make, and great to eat. Be prepared for lots of praise when you serve this one.*

**CAKE**
3 pounds cream cheese, softened
1½ cups granulated sugar
6 eggs
1 cup sour cream

1½ teaspoons vanilla extract
1½ teaspoons powdered sugar

**PAN**
10-inch springform pan

In a large bowl, beat the cream cheese and sugar until smooth. Add the eggs, one at a time, beating well after each addition. Add the sour cream and vanilla and continue to beat until smooth. Pour into a well-buttered springform pan. Place the pan inside of a larger pan containing 1 inch of water and bake in a preheated 400°F oven for 1 hour. Transfer the cake to a wire rack and allow to cool for 3 hours. Remove the sides of the springform pan and refrigerate the cake overnight. Remove the cheesecake from the refrigerator 1 hour before serving. Sprinkle the top of the cake with the powdered sugar shortly before serving.

———

# ENGLISH MOCHA
# CHEESECAKE

*An elegant addition to the dinner table or buffet, this cake boasts a vanilla wafer crust, a cream cheese and ricotta cheese filling that's been flavored with a mocha of cocoa and freeze-dried coffee, and a topping of whipped cream and finely chopped hazelnuts. A cake to indulge your guests.*

**CRUST**

1 cup vanilla wafer crumbs
1 tablespoon granulated sugar
2 tablespoons sweet butter, softened

**FILLING**

1 pound cream cheese, softened
¾ pound ricotta cheese
1¼ cups granulated sugar
6 tablespoons (¾ stick) sweet butter, softened
¼ cup all-purpose flour, sifted
1 teaspoon vanilla extract
1 teaspoon lemon juice
4 eggs
1 cup sour cream
1½ tablespoons freeze-dried instant coffee
2 teaspoons unsweetened cocoa
2 tablespoons hot water

**TOPPING**

1 cup heavy cream
1 tablespoon granulated sugar
½ cup finely chopped hazelnuts

**PAN**

9-inch springform pan

CRUST   In a small mixing bowl, combine the vanilla wafer crumbs, sugar, and butter. Blend well with fingers, fork, or pastry blender. Press or pat the mixture onto the bottom of a well-buttered springform pan. Chill in the freezer or refrigerator for about 30 minutes.

FILLING   In a large bowl, beat the cream cheese, ricotta cheese, sugar, butter, flour, vanilla, lemon juice, and eggs until very smooth. Fold in the sour cream. In a small bowl, mix the instant coffee and cocoa with the hot water until it becomes a paste. Add the coffee-cocoa paste to the cream cheese mixture and beat well until very smooth and creamy. Pour the mixture into the chilled springform pan and bake in a preheated 325°F oven for 1 hour. When done, turn off the oven and leave the cake in the closed oven for about 1½ hours.

TOPPING   Carefully remove the sides of the springform pan after the cake has cooled completely. In a small mixing bowl, whip the heavy cream with the sugar and spread this on top of the cake. Decorate by sprinkling the chopped hazelnuts on top of the whipped cream. Transfer the cake to a serving dish and either serve immediately or refrigerate.

# FRENCH APRICOT CHEESECAKE

*The crust of gingersnaps and finely chopped almonds,*
*moistened with apricot preserve, holds a light and creamy*
*cream cheese filling delicately flavored with apricot brandy and*
*crushed apricots, and topped with sour cream and*
*sliced apricots. A concoction to please the palate of the most*
*discerning cheesecake devotee.*

**CRUST**
1½ cups gingersnap crumbs
¼ cup granulated sugar
¼ cup finely chopped almonds
6 tablespoons (¾ stick) sweet butter, softened

**FILLING**
½ cup apricot preserve
1½ pounds cream cheese, softened
½ cup granulated sugar
3 eggs
1 teaspoon vanilla extract
¼ cup apricot brandy
½ cup heavy cream
2 cups chopped or crushed canned apricots, drained

**TOPPING**
1½ cups sour cream
1 tablespoon granulated sugar
1 cup canned apricots, drained and sliced

**PAN**
9-inch springform pan

**CRUST**   In a medium-size bowl, combine the gingersnap crumbs, sugar, chopped almonds, and butter. Blend well with fingers, fork, or pastry blender. Press or pat the mixture onto the bottom and sides of a well-buttered springform pan. Chill in the freezer or refrigerator for 30 minutes.

**FILLING**   In a small pan, heat the apricot preserve for 2 minutes (to liquify somewhat) then strain it. Pour onto the chilled gingersnap crust. In a large bowl, beat the cream cheese, sugar, and eggs until very smooth. Add the vanilla, apricot brandy, and heavy cream and continue to beat until smooth. Gently fold in the chopped or crushed apricots. Pour the mixture into the chilled pan. Place the springform pan inside of a larger pan containing 1 inch of water and bake in a preheated 325°F oven for 1½ hours. Transfer the cake to a wire rack and allow to cool for 30 minutes.

TOPPING   In a small mixing bowl, beat the sour cream and sugar until smooth. Spread the mixture evenly over the top of the cake and bake in a preheated 350° oven for 5 minutes. Transfer to a wire rack and allow to cool completely. Remove the sides of the springform pan and decorate the top of the cake with the sliced apricots. Refrigerate overnight. Remove from the refrigerator at least 2 hours before serving.

# FRENCH ORANGE RICOTTA CHEESECAKE

*For this cake, it's a pâte sucrée (sweet dough) shell, with a light, moist ricotta cheese filling, flavored with ground hazelnuts and rum, topped with fresh orange slices and honey— a visual and culinary feast.*

**SHELL**
1½ cups all-purpose flour, sifted
¼ cup granulated sugar
¼ pound (1 stick) sweet butter, softened
1 egg

**FILLING**
2 pounds ricotta cheese
½ cup granulated sugar
3 egg yolks
1 whole egg
1 cup heavy cream
¼ cup ground hazelnuts
2 tablespoons light rum
2 tablespoons lemon juice
⅛ teaspoon salt

**TOPPING**
½ cup honey
4 fresh oranges, peeled and finely sliced
1 teaspoon lemon juice

**PAN**
9-inch springform pan

**SHELL** In a large bowl, combine the flour, sugar, butter, and egg. Blend well with fingers, fork, or pastry blender. Form the dough into a ball, knead lightly with the heel of the hand against a smooth surface for a few seconds, then reform it into a ball. Wrap it in wax paper and chill in the refrigerator for 1 hour. When chilled, roll out the dough on a floured surface until ⅛ inch thick. Fit the dough into the springform pan, pressing it 2 inches up the sides of the pan and crimping the edge decoratively. Prick the bottom of the shell with a fork and chill in the freezer or refrigerator for 30 minutes. Next, line the shell with wax paper, fill it with uncooked rice or dried beans, and bake it in a preheated 350°F oven for 10 minutes. Carefully remove the rice and wax paper and bake the shell for another 10 to 15 minutes more, or until golden brown. Transfer to a wire rack and allow to cool completely.

FILLING   In a large bowl, beat the ricotta cheese, sugar, and egg yolks until very smooth. Add the whole egg, heavy cream, hazelnuts, rum, lemon juice, and salt and continue to beat until very smooth and creamy. Pour the mixture into the chilled shell and bake in a preheated 350° oven for 1 hour. Transfer to a wire rack and allow to cool thoroughly. Remove the sides of the springform pan and transfer the cake to a serving dish.

TOPPING   In a large bowl, combine most of the honey with the orange slices. Add the lemon juice and mix well. Arrange the orange slices decoratively over the top of the cake, and just before serving, brush the oranges with the remaining honey as a glaze.

# FRENCH-STYLE MAPLE–ALMOND CHEESECAKE

*A delicate pastry shell, a light and smooth cream cheese filling flavored with maple syrup, chopped almonds, raisins, and bourbon, and topped with fresh whipped cream and finely chopped walnuts—voilà! A gourmet's delight.*

**SHELL**
2 cups all-purpose flour, sifted
½ teaspoon salt
2 tablespoons granulated sugar
1 teaspoon baking powder
10 tablespoons (1¼ sticks) sweet butter, chilled
6 tablespoons heavy cream, lightly beaten with 1 egg yolk

**FILLING**
1½ pounds cream cheese, softened
3 ounces finely chopped almonds
3 whole eggs
1 egg white
1 cup sour cream
¾ cup maple syrup
3 tablespoons sweet butter, melted
2 tablespoons cornstarch
½ cup seedless raisins
¼ cup bourbon

**TOPPING**
1 cup heavy cream, whipped
½ cup finely chopped walnuts

**PAN**
9-inch springform pan

**SHELL**   In a large bowl, combine the flour, salt, sugar, baking powder, butter, and heavy cream. Blend well with fingers, fork, or pastry blender. Form the dough into a ball, knead lightly with the heel of the hand against a smooth surface for about 15 seconds, then reform it into a ball. Wrap it in wax paper and chill in the refrigerator for 1 hour. When chilled, roll out the dough on a floured surface until ³⁄₁₆ inch thick. Fit the dough into the springform pan, pressing it 2 inches up the sides of the pan and crimping the edge decoratively. Chill in the refrigerator or freezer for 30 minutes. Next, line the shell with wax paper, fill it with uncooked rice or dried beans, and bake it in a preheated 400°F oven for 8 minutes. Remove the rice and wax paper, prick the bottom of the shell all over with a fork, and bake it for 8 to 10 minutes more. Transfer to a wire rack and allow to cool for 30 minutes.

FILLING In a large bowl, beat the cream cheese, chopped almonds, eggs, egg white, sour cream, maple syrup, melted butter, and cornstarch until smooth and creamy. In a small saucepan, bring the raisins and bourbon to a simmer. Remove from the heat, allowing the raisins to macerate a few moments, then stir the raisins and bourbon into the cream cheese mixture. Pour into the chilled shell. Bake in a preheated 400° oven for 15 minutes, then reduce the temperature to 350° and continue to bake for 30 minutes more. Transfer to a wire rack and allow to cool completely. Carefully remove the sides of the springform pan and decorate the top of the cake with the whipped cream and chopped walnuts. Transfer to a serving dish and either serve immediately or refrigerate.

# NAPOLEON CHEESECAKE

*The little emperor would have loved this cheesecake.
Just a simple one, very smooth and custardy, that will delight
your palate. Serve it plain or with a sprinkling of powdered
sugar, and you'll find that one slice is not enough.*

**CAKE**

1 pound cream cheese,
   softened
1 pound creamed cottage
   cheese
1½ cups granulated
   sugar
4 eggs
1 teaspoon lemon juice

3 tablespoons flour, sifted
3 tablespoons cornstarch
1 teaspoon vanilla extract
¼ pound (1 stick) sweet
   butter, melted
1 cup sour cream
1½ teaspoons powdered
   sugar

**PAN**      9-inch springform pan

In a large bowl, beat the cream cheese, cottage cheese, sugar, and eggs until very smooth. Add the lemon juice, flour, cornstarch, vanilla, butter, and sour cream and continue beating the mixture until very smooth and creamy. Pour into a well-buttered springform pan and bake in a preheated 350°F oven for 1 hour. Then turn off the oven and let it sit in the closed oven for 2 hours. Transfer the cake to a wire rack and allow to cool completely. Carefully remove the sides of the springform pan and transfer the cake to a serving dish. Decorate the top of the cake by sprinkling some powdered sugar on it. Refrigerate the cake until ready to serve.

# GEORGIAN CHEESECAKE

*A vanilla wafer crust; a light, moist, very creamy filling flavored with a hint of lime and topped with peach pie filling— this is a long-standing favorite down South.*

**CRUST**  1 cup vanilla wafer crumbs
¼ cup granulated sugar
2 tablespoons sweet butter, softened

**FILLING**  1½ pounds cream cheese, softened
1 cup sour cream
⅓ cup all-purpose flour, sifted
3 eggs, separated
⅛ teaspoon salt
1½ teaspoons grated lime rind
1 teaspoon lime juice

**TOPPING**  21 ounces canned peach pie filling and topping

**PAN**  9-inch springform pan

**CRUST**  In a small mixing bowl, combine the vanilla wafer crumbs, sugar, and butter. Blend well with fingers, fork, or pastry blender. Press or pat the mixture onto the bottom of a well-buttered springform pan. Chill in the freezer or refrigerator for about 30 minutes.

**FILLING**  In a large bowl, beat the cream cheese, sour cream, flour, and egg yolks until very smooth and creamy. Add the salt, grated lime rind, and lime juice and continue to beat until smooth. In a small mixing bowl, beat the egg whites until stiff, then fold them into the cheese mixture. Pour the entire mixture into the chilled pan and bake in a preheated 325°F oven for 1¼ hours. Transfer to a wire rack and allow to cool for about 30 minutes.

**TOPPING**  Spread the peach pie filling evenly over the top of the cake and bake in a preheated 350° oven for 5 minutes. Transfer to a wire rack and allow to cool completely. Carefully remove the sides of the springform pan and transfer the cake to a serving dish. Either serve immediately or refrigerate.

---

# GERMAN CHOCOLATE
# CHEESECAKE

*This is a popular choice among chocolate lovers: an extra light and creamy, dark chocolate cheesecake topped with fresh whipped cream and chocolate curls (thin cigarette rolls). Serve this cake as the hearty conclusion to an otherwise simple meal.*

**CRUST**
2 cups chocolate wafer crumbs
2 tablespoons granulated sugar
4 tablespoons ( ½ stick) sweet butter, softened

**FILLING**
1½ pounds cream cheese, softened
2 tablespoons cornstarch
1 cup sour cream
1 teaspoon almond extract
1 cup heavy cream
8 ounces dark semisweet baking chocolate, cut into bits
4 eggs, separated
¾ cup granulated sugar
⅛ teaspoon cream of tartar

**TOPPING**
1 cup heavy cream, whipped
1 ounce semisweet baking chocolate, to make 6 chocolate curls, 2 inches long each

**PAN**
9-inch springform pan

CRUST  In a medium-size bowl, combine the chocolate wafer crumbs, sugar, and butter. Blend well with fingers, fork, or pastry blender. Press or pat the mixture onto the bottom and sides of a well-buttered springform pan. Chill in the freezer or refrigerator for about 30 minutes.

FILLING  In a large bowl, beat the cream cheese, cornstarch, sour cream, and almond extract until smooth. In small saucepan, scald the heavy cream, then remove from the heat and allow to cool for about 5 minutes. Add the chocolate bits and stir until the chocolate is completely melted. With a wire whisk, beat the mixture until it is cooled and light in texture. In a large bowl, with a whisk beat the egg yolks and ½ cup of the sugar until very thick and smooth. Add the chocolate mixture to the egg mixture and beat until everything has been smoothly combined. Then add the cream cheese mixture to the chocolate mixture and beat again until very smooth. In a separate bowl, beat the egg whites with the cream of tartar and the remaining ¼ cup sugar until the egg whites hold their peaks. Fold the egg whites into the cheese mixture and pour the entire mixture into the chilled shell. Place the springform pan inside of a larger pan containing 1 inch of water and bake in a preheated 300°F oven for 1½ hours. Transfer to a wire rack and allow to cool completely.

TOPPING  Prepare chocolate curls by melting the chocolate, spreading it thinly on a sheet of wax paper, and refrigerating for 30 minutes. Then with a flat knife scrape the chilled chocolate into curls and cut them into 2-inch-long sticks. Carefully remove the sides of the springform pan. Decorate by spreading the whipped cream evenly over the top of the cake and then adding the chocolate curls. Transfer the cake to a serving dish and serve.

# KÄSEKUCHEN GERMAN CHEESECAKE

*This traditional favorite may be found on the menus of many German restaurants. Made of a delicate pastry shell; a light, smooth cottage cheese filling flavored with raisins, currants, lemon rind, and chopped almonds; and a simple sprinkling of powdered sugar—it will become a traditional favorite with your guests as well.*

**SHELL**

1½ cups all-purpose flour, sifted
¼ cup granulated sugar
¼ pound (1 stick) sweet butter, softened
1 egg

**FILLING**

½ cup granulated sugar
½ cup seedless raisins
½ cup dried currants
2 large eggs
4 tablespoons (½ stick) sweet butter, melted
1½ tablespoons all-purpose flour, sifted
2 teaspoons grated lemon rind
½ teaspoon vanilla extract
2 pounds creamed cottage cheese
1 cup sour cream
1 cup finely chopped blanched almonds
1½ teaspoons powdered sugar

**PAN**      9-inch springform pan

**SHELL**   In a large bowl, combine the flour, sugar, butter, and egg. Blend well with fingers, fork, or pastry blender. Form the dough into a ball, knead lightly with the heel of the hand against a smooth surface for a few seconds, then reform it into a ball. Wrap it in wax paper and chill in the refrigerator for 1 hour. When chilled, roll out the dough on a floured surface until ⅛ inch thick. Fit the dough into the springform pan, pressing it 2 inches up the sides of the pan and crimping the edge decoratively. Prick the bottom of the shell with a fork and chill for 1 hour.

FILLING   In a large bowl, combine the sugar, raisins, currants, eggs, melted butter, flour, grated lemon rind, vanilla, cottage cheese, and sour cream. Beat until very smooth and creamy. Pour the mixture into the chilled shell and sprinkle the top with the chopped almonds. Bake in a preheated 375°F oven for 1 hour. Transfer the cake to a wire rack and allow to cool completely. Decorate the top of the cake with the powdered sugar, then remove the sides of the springform pan and serve.

---

# HAWAIIAN MANDARIN ORANGE CHEESECAKE

*A suggestion from the Hawaiian Islands, this delicate, creamy cheesecake with its hint of orange flavoring and the sweet tang of mandarin oranges, provides a mildly rich-flavored cheesecake, perfect after a special dinner.*

| | | |
|---|---|---|
| CRUST | 2 cups vanilla wafer crumbs<br>¼ cup granulated sugar | 6 tablespoons (¾ stick) sweet butter, softened |
| FILLING | 1½ pounds cream cheese, softened<br>2 eggs | ½ cup granulated sugar<br>1 teaspoon vanilla extract<br>1 teaspoon orange extract |
| TOPPING | 2 cups sour cream<br>7 tablespoons granulated sugar<br>11 ounces canned | mandarin oranges, with syrup<br>1 tablespoon cornstarch<br>½ cup finely chopped macadamia nuts |
| PAN | 9-inch springform pan | |

CRUST    In a medium-size bowl, combine the vanilla wafer crumbs, sugar, and butter. Blend well with fingers, fork, or pastry blender. Press or pat the mixture onto the bottom and sides of a well-buttered springform pan. Chill in the freezer or refrigerate for about 30 minutes.

FILLING    In a large bowl, beat the cream cheese, eggs, sugar, vanilla, and orange extract until very smooth and creamy. Pour the mixture into the chilled pan. Place the springform pan inside of a larger pan containing 1 inch of water and bake in a pre-heated 325°F oven for 1½ hours. Transfer the cake to a wire rack and allow to cool for at least 2 hours.

TOPPING    In a medium-size bowl, beat the sour cream and 3 tablespoons of the sugar until smooth, then spread the mixture evenly over the top of the cake and chill for 1 hour in the refrigerator. Over a small bowl, drain the mandarin oranges, reserving both the syrup and the oranges. In a small saucepan, combine ⅓ cup syrup, the remaining 4 tablespoons sugar, and the cornstarch. Cook for 3 to 5 minutes, stirring occasionally, over medium heat until the mixture thickens. Let the glaze cool for about 5 minutes. Spread the glaze over the top of the cake and chill for another 45 minutes. Carefully remove the sides of the springform pan and decorate the top of the cake with the mandarin orange slices and the macadamia nuts. Transfer the cake to a serving dish and serve.

# IRISH CHEESECAKE

*A fine example of Irish dessert-making: a superb pastry shell,
a smooth and delicate filling flavored with lemon and raisins, and
topped with whipped cream. From its appearance, no one will
suspect that this is a cheesecake—until it's served and enjoyed.*

**SHELL**
1½ cups all-purpose flour, sifted
¼ cup granulated sugar
¼ pound (1 stick) sweet butter, softened
1 egg

**FILLING**
2 pounds creamed cottage cheese
2 eggs, separated
2 tablespoons granulated sugar
1 tablespoon sweet butter, melted
2 tablespoons lemon juice
2 teaspoons grated lemon rind
½ teaspoon vanilla extract
⅛ teaspoon cream of tartar
½ cup seedless raisins

**TOPPING**
1 cup heavy cream, whipped

**PAN**
9-inch springform pan

**SHELL**   In a large bowl, combine the flour, sugar, butter, and egg. Blend well with fingers, fork, or pastry blender. Form the dough into a ball, knead lightly with the heel of the hand against a smooth surface for a few seconds, then reform it into a ball. Wrap it in wax paper and chill in the refrigerator for 1 hour. When chilled, roll out the dough on a floured surface until ⅛ inch thick. Fit the dough into the springform pan, pressing it 2 inches up the sides of the pan and crimping the edge decoratively. Prick the bottom of the shell with a fork and chill in the freezer or refrigerator for 30 minutes. Next, line the shell with wax paper, fill it with uncooked rice or dried beans, and bake it in a preheated 350°F oven for 10 minutes. Carefully remove the rice and wax paper and bake the shell for another 10 minutes. Transfer to a wire rack and allow to cool for about 30 minutes.

FILLING   In a large bowl, beat the cottage cheese, egg yolks, and sugar until very smooth. Add the melted butter, lemon juice, grated lemon rind, and vanilla and continue to beat until smooth. In a small mixing bowl, beat the egg whites and cream of tartar until the whites hold their peaks. Fold them into the cottage cheese mixture. Mix in the raisins, then pour the mixture into the chilled springform pan and bake in a preheated 350° oven for 45 minutes. Transfer the cake to a wire rack and allow to cool completely.

TOPPING   Carefully remove the sides of the springform pan and decorate the top of the cake by spreading the whipped cream on top. Transfer to a serving dish and either serve immediately or refrigerate.

---

# ISRAELI CHEESECAKE

*This cheesecake is a light, smooth blending of pot cheese,*
*yogurt, and sour cream. These traditional dairy favorites, flavored*
*with raisins and a taste of honey, form a creation*
*"much sweeter than wine."*

| | | |
|---|---|---|
| CAKE | 1½ pounds pot cheese | 1 teaspoon vanilla extract |
| | ¾ cup granulated sugar | 1 cup seedless raisins |
| | 3 eggs | ½ cup honey |
| | 1 cup plain yogurt | 1½ teaspoons powdered |
| | 1 cup sour cream | sugar |
| PAN | 9-inch springform pan | |

In a large bowl, beat the pot cheese, sugar, eggs, and yogurt until very smooth. Add the sour cream and vanilla and continue to beat until smooth and creamy. In a small skillet, combine the raisins and honey and heat until the raisins are fully coated with the honey. Fold the raisin and honey mixture into the cheese mixture. Pour into a well-buttered springform pan and bake in a preheated 400°F oven for 30 minutes, then reduce the temperature to 325° and continue to bake for another hour. Transfer to a wire rack and allow to cool completely. Carefully remove the sides of the springform pan and decorate the top of the cake with the powdered sugar. Refrigerate for at least 2 to 3 hours before serving.

---

# ITALIAN CIOCCOLATA
# CHEESECAKE

*Truly an Italian delicacy—a ricotta and chocolate cheesecake,*
*topped only with a dusting of powdered sugar. It's ideal*
*to serve as the "dolce" to conclude an Italian-style dinner.*

| CAKE | 2 pounds ricotta cheese | 3 tablespoons |
|------|-------------------------|---------------|
|      | ¼ cup heavy cream       | unsweetened cocoa |
|      | 4 eggs                  | ¾ cup granulated sugar |
|      | ¼ cup light rum         | 1½ teaspoons powdered |
|      | 1 teaspoon chocolate    | sugar |
|      | flavoring               | |

| PAN | 9-inch springform pan |
|-----|-----------------------|

In a large bowl, beat the ricotta cheese, heavy cream, eggs, rum, chocolate flavoring, cocoa, and sugar until very smooth and creamy. Pour the mixture into a well-buttered springform pan and bake in a preheated 400°F oven for 30 minutes, then reduce the temperature to 325° and continue to bake for another hour, or until golden brown. Transfer to a wire rack and allow to cool completely. When completely cooled, remove the sides of the springform pan and decorate the top of the cake with the powdered sugar. Either refrigerate or serve immediately.

---

# ITALIAN EASTER
# CHEESECAKE

*This is an Italian Easter favorite—Buona Pasqua! Its delicate pastry shell and ricotta cheese filling, pleasantly flavored with orange rind and citron and topped with powdered sugar, make it a special choice to complement an Italian meal.*

| | | |
|---|---|---|
| **SHELL** | 1½ cups all-purpose flour, sifted<br>¼ cup granulated sugar | ¼ pound (1 stick) sweet butter, softened<br>1 egg |
| **FILLING** | 2 pounds ricotta cheese<br>4 egg whites, beaten stiff<br>½ cup granulated sugar<br>1 teaspoon vanilla extract<br>2 tablespoons grated orange rind | 2 tablespoons finely chopped citron<br>1½ teaspoons powdered sugar |
| **PAN** | 9-inch springform pan | |

**SHELL** In a large bowl, combine the flour, sugar, butter, and egg. Blend well with fingers, fork, or pastry blender. Form the dough into a ball, knead lightly with the heel of the hand against a smooth surface for a few seconds, then reform it into a ball. Wrap it in wax paper and chill in the refrigerator for 1 hour. When chilled, roll out the dough on a floured surface until ⅛ inch thick. Fit the dough into the springform pan, pressing it 2 inches up the sides of the pan and crimping the edge decoratively. Prick the bottom of the shell with a fork and chill in the freezer or refrigerator for 30 minutes. Next, line the shell with wax paper, fill it with uncooked rice or dried beans, and bake it in a preheated 350°F oven for 10 minutes. Carefully remove the rice and wax paper and bake the shell for another 10 minutes more, or until golden brown. Transfer to a wire rack and allow to cool for about 30 minutes.

FILLING  In a large bowl, beat the ricotta cheese, sugar, and vanilla until creamy and smooth and then fold in the egg whites until mixture is fully blended. Add the orange rind and citron, mixing until very smooth. Pour into the chilled pan and bake in a preheated 350° oven for 1¼ hours. Transfer to a wire rack and allow to cool completely. Decorate the top of the cake by sprinkling the powdered sugar on it. Either refrigerate or serve immediately. Remove the sides of the springform pan before serving.

# ITALIAN HOLIDAY
# CHEESECAKE

*A luscious-tasting cheesecake that is the pride of the Italian
baker. There are many variations of the classic, but this recipe
is the most practical and most widely enjoyed. It uses
ricotta cheese delicately flavored with rum and lemon and orange
rinds, and its handsome golden-brown top is sprinkled
with powdered sugar.*

| | | |
|---|---|---|
| CRUST | 1 cup graham cracker crumbs | 2 tablespoons sweet butter, softened |
| | 1 tablespoon granulated sugar | |
| FILLING | 2 pounds ricotta cheese | rind of 1 lemon, grated |
| | 4 eggs | rind of 1 orange, grated |
| | ¾ cup granulated sugar | 1½ teaspoons powdered sugar |
| | ¼ cup light rum | |
| | 1 teaspoon vanilla extract | |
| PAN | 9-inch springform pan | |

CRUST   In a small mixing bowl, combine the graham cracker
crumbs, sugar, and butter. Blend well with fingers, fork, or pastry
blender. Press or pat the mixture onto the bottom of a well-
buttered springform pan, then chill in the freezer or refrigerator
for 30 minutes.

FILLING   In a large bowl, beat the ricotta cheese, eggs, sugar,
rum, vanilla, and grated lemon and orange rinds with a spoon
until very smooth and creamy. Pour into the chilled pan and
bake in a preheated 400°F oven for 30 minutes, then reduce the
temperature to 325° and bake for 1 hour more. Transfer to a wire

rack and allow to cool completely. Refrigerate overnight. Do not remove the sides of the pan until ready to serve. Sprinkle the top of the cake with the powdered sugar before serving.

———

# MARYLAND CHEESECAKE

*This is the perfect dessert to offer your party guests—*
*simple to make, light and delicate, with a tasteful and attractive*
*appearance. Since the batter has a bit of flour in it, be careful*
*not to leave it in the oven too long, which tends to make*
*it dry and heavy rather than delicate.*

**CRUST**
2 cups gingersnap crumbs
½ cup granulated sugar
1 teaspoon ground cinnamon
¼ pound (1 stick) sweet butter, melted

**FILLING**
4 eggs
1 cup granulated sugar
⅛ teaspoon salt
1½ teaspoons lemon juice
1½ teaspoons grated lemon rind
1 cup heavy cream
1½ pounds creamed cottage cheese
3 tablespoons flour
¼ cup mixed chopped nuts (walnuts, hazelnuts, pecans)
1½ teaspoons powdered sugar

**PAN**
9-inch springform pan

**CRUST**  In a medium-size bowl, combine the gingersnap crumbs, sugar, cinnamon, and butter. Blend well with fingers, fork, or pastry blender. Press or pat 1¼ cups of the mixture onto the bottom of a well-buttered springform pan. Chill in the freezer or refrigerator for 15 minutes.

FILLING   In a large bowl, beat the eggs and sugar until light and smooth. Add the salt, lemon juice, lemon rind, heavy cream, cottage cheese, and flour and beat the mixture thoroughly. Strain the mixture through a fine sieve. Pour into the chilled pan and sprinkle the chopped nuts and the remaining gingersnap crumb mixture on top of the cake. Bake in a preheated 350°F oven for 1 hour, then turn off the oven, open the door, and let the cake stand in the open oven for 1 hour. Transfer to a wire rack to cool completely. Refrigerate overnight. Before serving, carefully remove the sides of the springform pan and sprinkle the top of the cake with the powdered sugar. For best results, remove the cheesecake from the refrigerator about 2 hours before serving.

---

# NEW ENGLAND CREAM CHEESECAKE

*Lots of eggs for this one! A luxurious choice for entertaining a large group, it will serve twelve to sixteen people. The plain sour cream topping can easily be decorated to celebrate a birthday or anniversary.*

| | | |
|---|---|---|
| CRUST | 3½ cups graham cracker crumbs | ¾ cup (1½ sticks) sweet butter, melted |
| FILLING | 3 pounds cream cheese, softened | 1½ teaspoons vanilla extract |
| | 2 cups granulated sugar | 12 eggs |
| TOPPING | 3 cups sour cream | 1½ teaspoons vanilla extract |
| | 6 tablespoons granulated sugar | |
| PAN | 10-inch springform pan | |

CRUST   In a large bowl, combine the graham cracker crumbs and butter. Blend well with fingers, fork, or pastry blender. Press or pat the mixture onto the bottom and sides of a well-buttered springform pan. Chill in the freezer or refrigerator for about 30 minutes.

FILLING   In a large bowl, beat the cream cheese, sugar, and vanilla until smooth. Beat in the eggs, one at a time, making sure that the mixture is smooth. Pour into the chilled springform pan and bake in a preheated 375°F oven for 1 hour. Remove the cake from the oven and place it on a wire rack to cool for about 30 minutes.

TOPPING   In a medium-size bowl, combine the sour cream, sugar, and vanilla and beat until smooth. Spread the mixture evenly over the top of the cake and bake in a preheated 475° oven for 5 minutes. Transfer the cake to a wire rack and allow to cool for 2 hours. Remove the sides of the springform pan and refrigerate the cake overnight. Remove the cake from the refrigerator at least 2 hours before serving.

# RUSSIAN PASKHA
# CHEESECAKE

*This Russian fruit cheesecake, served at Eastertime and considered a holiday treat, consists of a cottage cheese filling flavored with raisins, almonds, diced glacéed fruit, and whole glacéed cherries. Serve this anytime you're celebrating— it looks so elegant and festive on buffet or dinner table.*

CAKE

3 pounds creamed cottage cheese
½ pound (2 sticks) sweet butter, softened
1 cup granulated sugar
3 eggs
1 teaspoon vanilla extract
½ cup sour cream
½ cup seedless raisins

½ cup finely chopped blanched almonds
1 cup whole blanched almonds
½ cup diced mixed glacéed fruit
½ cup glacéed cherries
1½ teaspoons powdered sugar

PAN

10-inch springform pan

In a large bowl, beat the cottage cheese, butter, sugar, and eggs until very smooth and creamy. Add the vanilla and sour cream and continue to beat until smooth. Fold in the raisins, chopped and whole almonds, glacéed fruits, and glacéed cherries. Pour the mixture into a well-buttered springform pan and bake in a preheated 350°F oven for 45 minutes. Transfer to a wire rack and allow to cool completely. Refrigerate overnight. Carefully remove the sides of the springform pan, decorate the top of the cake with the powdered sugar, and serve.

# SAN FRANCISCO HONEY AND SPICE CHEESECAKE

*The very moist and creamy filling is flavored with dark honey, ground cloves, allspice, and freeze-dried coffee to make this a decidedly special cheesecake. Topped with powdered sugar or whipped cream, it is a delectable choice for special occasions.*

**CAKE**

1½ pounds cream cheese, softened
½ cup dark honey
3 eggs
1 teaspoon vanilla extract
3 tablespoons all-purpose flour, sifted
1 tablespoon cornstarch
½ cup heavy cream
½ teaspoon ground cloves
1 teaspoon allspice
1 tablespoon instant freeze-dried coffee, dissolved in 1 teaspoon hot water
1½ teaspoons powdered sugar (optional)
1 cup heavy cream, whipped (optional)

**PAN**    9-inch springform pan

In a large bowl, beat the cream cheese, honey, and eggs until very smooth. Add the vanilla, flour, and cornstarch and continue to beat until very smooth. Add the heavy cream, cloves, and allspice and beat well. Add the coffee paste to the cheese mixture and beat until very smooth. Pour into a well-buttered springform pan and bake in a preheated 325°F oven for 1 hour. When done, turn off the oven and allow the cake to remain in the closed oven for 20 minutes. Transfer to a wire rack and allow to cool completely. Carefully remove the sides of the springform pan and transfer the cake to a serving dish. If desired, decorate the top of the cake with the powdered sugar or whipped cream and serve.

# SCOTTISH ALMOND CHEESECAKE

*This cake, a light, refreshing finale to a hearty dinner, consists of a delicate crust of vanilla wafer crumbs and finely chopped almonds, a light and creamy almond-flavored filling topped with sour cream (also flavored with a hint of almond) and decorated with whipped cream and whole toasted almonds.*

**CRUST**
1 cup vanilla wafer crumbs
1 cup finely chopped blanched almonds
3 tablespoons granulated sugar
6 tablespoons ( ¾ stick) sweet butter, softened

**FILLING**
1 pound cream cheese, softened
¾ cup granulated sugar
3 large eggs (or 4 medium-size eggs)
1¼ teaspoons almond extract
⅛ teaspoon salt
½ cup ground blanched almonds

**TOPPING**
1 cup sour cream
3 tablespoons granulated sugar
½ teaspoon vanilla extract
½ teaspoon almond extract
1 cup heavy cream, whipped
½ cup blanched whole almonds, toasted

**PAN**  9-inch springform pan

**CRUST** In a medium-size bowl, combine the vanilla wafer crumbs, chopped almonds, sugar, and butter. Blend well with fingers, fork, or pastry blender. Press or pat the mixture onto the bottom and halfway up the sides of a well-buttered springform pan. Chill in the freezer or refrigerator for about 30 minutes.

FILLING   In a large bowl, beat the cream cheese, sugar, and eggs until very smooth. Add the almond extract and salt and continue to beat until smooth. Stir in the ground almonds until very smooth and creamy. Pour the mixture into the chilled pan and bake in the middle of a preheated 350°F oven for 45 minutes. Transfer to a wire rack and allow to cool for 30 minutes.

TOPPING   In a small mixing bowl, beat the sour cream, sugar, vanilla, and almond extract until smooth. Spread the mixture evenly over the top of the cake and bake in a preheated 350° oven for 7 minutes. Transfer to a wire rack and allow to cool for 3 hours. Carefully remove the sides of the springform pan and decorate the cake with the whipped cream and toasted almonds. Transfer to a serving dish and either serve immediately or refrigerate.

# SWEDISH RUM CHEESECAKE

*Characterized by the Swedish touch of blending three cheeses—
cream cheese, cottage cheese, and ricotta cheese—and
lightly flavored with dark rum and lemon rind and topped
with a dusting of powdered sugar, this cheesecake is a delight.*

CRUST

1 cup gingersnap crumbs
1 tablespoon granulated
sugar

2 tablespoons sweet
butter, softened

FILLING

1 pound cream cheese,
softened
1 pound creamed cottage
cheese
1 pound ricotta cheese
6 eggs
1¼ cups granulated
sugar

1 teaspoon vanilla extract
3 ounces dark rum
3 teaspoons rum extract
rind of 1 lemon, grated
1½ teaspoons powdered
sugar

PAN      10-inch springform pan

CRUST  In a small mixing bowl, combine the gingersnap crumbs, sugar, and butter. Blend well with fingers, fork, or pastry blender. Press or pat the mixture onto the bottom of a well-buttered springform pan. Chill in the freezer or refrigerator for about 30 minutes.

FILLING  In a large bowl, beat the cream cheese, cottage cheese, ricotta cheese, eggs, and sugar until very smooth. Add the vanilla, rum, and rum extract and continue to beat until very smooth. Mix in the grated lemon rind. Pour the mixture into the chilled springform pan and bake in a preheated 400°F oven for 30 minutes, then reduce the temperature to 325° and bake for another hour. Transfer to a wire rack and allow to cool completely. Refrigerate overnight. Carefully remove the sides of the springform pan and transfer the cake to a serving dish. Decorate the top of the cake by sprinkling the powdered sugar on it, then serve.

---

# TRADITIONAL SICILIAN CHEESECAKE

*Molta deliziosa—another fine Italian cheesecake of ricotta cheese, this time flavored with orange, lemon, and anisette liqueur, a very popular Italian cordial. And, it's easy to prepare.*

**CAKE**

| | |
|---|---|
| 2 pounds ricotta cheese | ¼ cup anisette liqueur |
| ¾ cup granulated sugar | 3 tablespoons all-purpose |
| 4 eggs, separated | flour, sifted |
| 1 cup heavy cream | rind of 1 orange, grated |
| 1 teaspoon vanilla extract | rind of 1 lemon, grated |
| ¼ teaspoon salt | 1½ teaspoons powdered |
| | sugar |

**PAN**    9-inch springform pan

In a large bowl, beat the ricotta cheese, sugar, and egg yolks until smooth. Add the heavy cream, vanilla, salt, flour, and anisette and continue to beat until smooth and very creamy. Add the grated orange and lemon rinds and mix gently with a spoon. In a small mixing bowl, beat the egg whites until firm, then fold them into the cheesecake mixture. Pour into a well-buttered springform pan and bake in a preheated 350°F oven for 1 hour. When done, turn off the oven, open the door, and allow the cake to sit in the oven for 30 minutes. Transfer to a wire rack and allow to cool completely. Carefully remove the sides of the springform pan and decorate the top of the cake with the powdered sugar. Either refrigerate or serve immediately.

------

# SWISS CHOCOLATE
# CHEESECAKE

*An excellent dessert choice to follow a light lunch or dinner.
A simple, light, and creamy cheesecake, delicately flavored with
cocoa and chocolate flavoring—not too sweet.*

CAKE  1½ pounds cream cheese, softened
1 cup granulated sugar
4 eggs
½ cup heavy cream
1 teaspoon vanilla extract
½ teaspoon chocolate flavoring

3 tablespoons unsweetened cocoa
1½ tablespoons sweet butter, melted
1½ teaspoons powdered sugar

PAN  9-inch springform pan

In a large bowl, beat the cream cheese, sugar, and 1 egg until very smooth. Add the remaining 3 eggs, one at a time, making sure that the mixture is smooth after beating in each addition. Add the heavy cream, vanilla, and chocolate flavoring and continue to beat until smooth and creamy. In a skillet, blend the cocoa with the butter. Pour the chocolate mixture into the cheesecake mixture and beat until blended and very smooth. Pour into a well-buttered springform pan and then place the springform pan inside of a larger pan containing 1 inch of water. Bake in a preheated 325°F oven for 1½ hours. Transfer to a wire rack and allow to cool completely. Remove the sides of the springform pan and refrigerate overnight. Remove the cake from the refrigerator 2 hours before serving and decorate the top by sprinkling the powdered sugar on top of it.

---

# SWISS COCOA MARBLED CHEESECAKE

*A cheesecake for those who prefer the taste of bittersweet chocolate, blended lightly into the gentle sweetness of the cream cheese filling. An exciting and attractive cheesecake with its chocolate-marbled top.*

**CRUST**
1 cup graham cracker crumbs
¼ cup granulated sugar
3 tablespoons sweet butter, softened

**FILLING**
1½ pounds cream cheese, softened
1 cup granulated sugar
3 eggs
2 teaspoons vanilla extract
3 tablespoons all-purpose flour, sifted
2 tablespoons cornstarch
½ cup heavy cream
2 tablespoons sweet butter
2 tablespoons unsweetened Swiss cocoa

**PAN**
9-inch springform pan

**CRUST**  In a small mixing bowl, combine the graham cracker crumbs, sugar, and butter. Blend well with fingers, fork, or pastry blender. Press or pat the mixture onto the bottom of a well-buttered springform pan. Chill in the freezer or refrigerator for about 30 minutes.

FILLING    In a large bowl, beat the cream cheese, sugar, and eggs until very smooth. Add the vanilla, flour, cornstarch, and heavy cream and continue to beat until very smooth. In a small skillet, melt the butter and blend in the cocoa until smooth. Pour the cheese mixture into the chilled pan, then drop the cocoa mixture into the center of it and swirl it through with a knife. Bake in a preheated 325°F oven for 1 hour. Then turn off the oven and let the cake remain in the closed oven for 45 minutes. Transfer to a wire rack and allow to cool completely. Carefully remove the sides of the springform pan and transfer the cake to a serving dish. Either serve immediately or refrigerate.

# REFRIGERATOR
# CHEESECAKES

# Simple Cheesecakes

## SIMPLE REFRIGERATOR CHEESECAKE

*This is truly one of the easiest cheesecakes of all to make. Prepare a simple graham cracker crust, mix the cream cheese filling, refrigerate, and serve. It's rich, creamy, and a sensible choice in warm weather—a midsummer night's dream!*

**CRUST**
1⅔ cups graham cracker crumbs
¼ cup granulated sugar
¼ teaspoon vanilla extract
4 tablespoons (½ stick) sweet butter, softened

**FILLING**
1 pound cream cheese, softened
28 ounces canned sweetened condensed milk
⅔ cup lemon juice
2 teaspoons vanilla extract
21 ounces canned pie filling and topping (cherry, blueberry, strawberry, pineapple, etc.) (optional)

**PAN**
9-inch springform pan

**CRUST** In a medium-size bowl, combine the graham cracker crumbs, sugar, vanilla, and butter. Blend well with fingers, fork, or pastry blender. Press or pat the mixture onto the bottom of a well-buttered springform pan, then bake in a preheated 375°F

147

oven for 8 minutes. Transfer to a wire rack and allow to cool for at least 30 minutes.

FILLING  In a large bowl, beat the cream cheese and sweetened condensed milk until smooth. Add the lemon juice and vanilla and continue to beat until very smooth and creamy. Pour the mixture into the cooled springform pan. Refrigerate for 3 hours, or until set and firm. Either serve as is or spread the fruit pie filling and topping evenly over the top of the cheesecake and refrigerate for 2 more hours to set the topping. Remove from the refrigerator 1 hour before serving and carefully remove the sides of the springform pan.

# OLD-FASHIONED
# REFRIGERATOR CHEESECAKE

*While there are many variations of this cheesecake, this recipe is one of the easiest to prepare, and one of the most delicate tasting. The crust of this light, creamy smooth cake is made of zwieback crumbs with cinnamon. Lemon rind is folded into the batter.*

CRUST
2 cups zwieback crumbs
¼ cup granulated sugar
¼ pound (1 stick) sweet butter, melted
2 teaspoons ground cinnamon

FILLING
2 tablespoons unflavored gelatin
1 cup cold water
3 eggs, separated
½ cup granulated sugar
1 pound cream cheese, softened
3 tablespoons lemon juice
1 tablespoon grated lemon rind
¼ teaspoon salt
½ cup heavy cream

PAN
9-inch springform pan

CRUST  In a medium-size bowl, combine the zwieback crumbs, sugar, butter, and cinnamon. Blend well with fingers, fork, or pastry blender. Press or pat three-quarters of this crumb mixture onto the bottom of a well-buttered springform pan. Chill in the freezer or refrigerator for 30 minutes.

FILLING  Soak the gelatin in ½ cup of the cold water for 5 minutes. In a double boiler, heat the egg yolks, ½ cup of the sugar, and the remaining ½ cup of cold water, stirring constantly, until the mixture coats a metal spoon. Remove from heat. Add the softened gelatin and stir until completely dissolved. Add the cream cheese and beat until smooth. Add the lemon juice, grated lemon rind, and salt and beat until very smooth. Chill in the refrigerator for 1 hour. When cooled, remove the mixture from the refrigerator and beat well. In separate small mixing bowls, whip the heavy cream and beat egg whites until stiff, then fold both into the cheese mixture. Pour into the chilled pan, sprinkle the remaining crumbs over the top of the cake, and chill in the refrigerator for 3 hours, or until firm. Remove the sides of the springform pan and serve.

---

# AMERICAN REFRIGERATOR
# CHEESECAKE

*A grand old favorite—a simple zwieback crumb crust,
a light cottage cheese filling flavored with orange juice, and a
topping of gingersnap crumbs. Serve directly from the
refrigerator for a cool treat.*

| | | |
|---|---|---|
| **CRUST** | 1½ cups zwieback crumbs | 4 tablespoons (½ stick) sweet butter, softened |
| **FILLING** | 2 tablespoons unflavored gelatin | orange juice concentrate, thawed |
| | ¼ teaspoon salt | 3 cups creamed cottage cheese |
| | 1 cup granulated sugar | |
| | 2 eggs, separated | 1 cup heavy cream, whipped |
| | 6 ounces canned frozen | |
| **TOPPING** | 2 tablespoons sweet butter, melted | ½ cup gingersnap crumbs |
| **PAN** | 9-inch springform pan | |

CRUST  In a medium-size bowl, combine the zwieback crumbs and butter. Blend well with fingers, fork, or pastry blender. Press or pat the mixture onto the bottom of a well-buttered springform pan and chill in the refrigerator for 30 minutes.

FILLING  In a double boiler, mix the gelatin, salt, and ¾ cup of the sugar. Add the egg yolks and orange juice concentrate, then cook over boiling water, stirring constantly, until the gelatin mixture thickens (about 10 minutes). Remove from the heat and let cool. Put the cottage cheese through a sieve and add the cooled mixture. Chill the complete mixture for 15 minutes, stirring occasionally, until the mixture mounds slightly when dropped from the spoon. In a small mixing bowl, beat the egg whites until stiff, gradually adding the remaining ¼ cup sugar. Fold both the egg white mixture and the whipped cream into the gelatin and cottage cheese mixture. Pour into the springform pan.

TOPPING  Combine the butter and gingersnap crumbs and sprinkle this mixture over the top of the cake. Refrigerate until firm. Carefully remove the sides of the springform pan and serve.

# Chocolate Cheesecakes

## CHOCOLATE CHIP CHEESECAKE

*Take it easy with this quick and simple recipe—a chocolate wafer crust, a creamy cream cheese filling flavored with cocoa and tiny chocolate chips . . . and oh so easy on the eyes, too.*

**CRUST**
1 cup chocolate wafer crumbs
1 tablespoon granulated sugar
2 tablespoons sweet butter, softened

**FILLING**
3 tablespoons unflavored gelatin
½ cup cold water
3 eggs, separated
½ cup granulated sugar
¼ cup milk
1½ pounds cream cheese, softened
1 teaspoon vanilla extract
1 cup heavy cream
2 tablespoons sweet butter
¼ cup unsweetened cocoa
½ cup tiny chocolate morsels

**PAN**
10-inch springform pan

**CRUST**  In a small mixing bowl, combine the chocolate wafer crumbs, sugar, and butter. Blend well with fingers, fork, or pastry blender. Press or pat the mixture onto the bottom of a well-

152

buttered springform pan. Chill in the freezer or refrigerator for about 30 minutes.

FILLING   Soften the gelatin in the cold water. In a small saucepan, combine the egg yolks and sugar and gradually stir in the milk. Cook the mixture over medium heat, stirring, until it coats a metal spoon. Remove from the heat and stir in the gelatin. In a large bowl, beat the cream cheese until very smooth, then add the vanilla and continue to beat until smooth. Add the gelatin mixture to the cheese mixture and beat until very smooth. Chill in the refrigerator for 30 minutes or until the mixture is set. In separate small mixing bowls, whip the heavy cream and beat the egg whites until stiff, then fold both into the cheese mixture. In a small skillet, melt the butter and blend in the cocoa, then add the cocoa mixture to the cheese mixture and beat until very smooth. Stir in the chocolate morsels. Pour the mixture into the chilled springform pan and refrigerate for 3 hours, or until firm. Carefully remove the sides of the springform pan, transfer the cake to a serving dish, and serve.

# CHOCOLATE–CHERRY CHEESECAKE

*Not only a feast for the eyes, but a banquet for the taste buds as well. The delicate chocolate wafer crust, the creamy cream cheese filling flavored with chocolate, and the topping of luscious cherry pie filling will bring back memories of chocolate-covered cherries.*

CRUST
2 cups chocolate wafer crumbs
¼ cup granulated sugar

6 tablespoons (¾ stick) sweet butter, softened

FILLING
3 tablespoons unflavored gelatin
½ cup cold water
3 eggs, separated
¾ cup granulated sugar
½ cup light cream

1½ pounds cream cheese, softened
1 teaspoon vanilla extract
¼ cup unsweetened cocoa
1 cup heavy cream, whipped

TOPPING
21 ounces canned cherry pie filling and topping

PAN
10-inch springform pan

CRUST   In a medium-size bowl, combine the chocolate wafer crumbs, sugar, and butter. Blend well with fingers, fork, or pastry blender. Press or pat the mixture onto the bottom and sides of a well-buttered springform pan. Chill in the freezer or refrigerator for 30 minutes.

FILLING   Soften the gelatin in the cold water. In a small saucepan, combine the egg yolks and sugar and gradually stir in the light cream. Cook the mixture over medium heat, stirring until it coats a metal spoon. Remove from the heat and stir in the softened gelatin. In a large bowl, beat the cream cheese until smooth. Add the vanilla and cocoa and beat until very smooth. Add the gelatin mixture to the cheese mixture and beat until very smooth. Chill in the refrigerator for 30 minutes or until the mixture is set. In a small mixing bowl, beat the egg whites until stiff. Fold both the whipped cream and egg whites into the cheese mixture. Pour into the chilled springform pan, then refrigerate for 3 hours, or until firm.

TOPPING Spread the cherry pie filling evenly over the top of the cake. Return the cake to the refrigerator for 2 hours. When chilled, carefully remove the sides of the springform pan and transfer the cake to a serving dish.

# Coffee Cheesecakes

## CAFÉ AU LAIT CHEESECAKE

*Dedicated to light-coffee lovers, this recipe brings a new dimension to the familiar cheesecake: a crust of butter cookies combined with a soft cream cheese filling flavored with coffee liqueur and freeze-dried instant coffee. You may choose to top it off with fresh whipped cream. This cake can, if you wish, be prepared well in advance, kept frozen till wanted, then thawed to serve.*

**CRUST**
2 cups butter cookie crumbs
¼ cup granulated sugar

6 tablespoons (¾ stick) sweet butter, softened

**FILLING**
3 tablespoons unflavored gelatin
½ cup cold water
3 eggs, separated
½ cup granulated sugar
½ cup light cream
1½ pounds cream cheese, softened

1 teaspoon vanilla extract
1 cup heavy cream
2 teaspoons coffee liqueur
2 tablespoons freeze-dried instant coffee, dissolved in 3 tablespoons hot water

**PAN**
10-inch springform pan

**CRUST** In a medium-size bowl, combine the butter cookie crumbs, sugar, and butter. Blend well with fingers, fork, or pastry blender. Press or pat the mixture onto the bottom and sides of a well-buttered springform pan. Chill in the freezer or refrigerator for about 30 minutes.

FILLING  Soften the gelatin in the cold water. In a small saucepan, combine the egg yolks and sugar and gradually stir in the light cream. Cook the mixture over medium heat, stirring, until it coats a metal spoon. Remove from the heat and stir in the softened gelatin. Beat the cream cheese until very smooth and creamy, then add the vanilla and continue to beat until very smooth and creamy. Add the gelatin mixture to the cheese mixture and beat until smooth. Chill in the refrigerator for 30 minutes or until the mixture is set. In separate small mixing bowls, whip the heavy cream and beat the egg whites until stiff, then fold both into the cheese mixture. In a small saucepan, heat the instant coffee dissolved in water, and the coffee liqueur, stirring until smooth. Add the coffee mixture to the cheese mixture and beat until very smooth and creamy. Pour into the chilled springform pan and refrigerate for 3 hours, or until the cake is set and firm. Carefully remove the sides of the springform pan, transfer the cake to a serving dish, and serve.

# ESPRESSO CHEESECAKE

*Bravo! This attractive cake calls for a crust of chocolate wafers and a soft, creamy cream cheese filling flavored with coffee liqueur and espresso instant coffee, to be topped with chocolate curls and a sprinkling of cinnamon. Served directly from the refrigerator, it's a refreshing final course.*

**CRUST**
2 cups chocolate wafer crumbs
½ cup granulated sugar
6 tablespoons (¾ stick) sweet butter, softened

**FILLING**
2 tablespoons unflavored gelatin
½ cup coffee-flavored liqueur
½ cup water
3 eggs, separated
¼ cup granulated sugar
2 teaspoons instant Italian espresso coffee, dissolved in 1 tablespoon hot water
1 teaspoon ground cinnamon
¼ teaspoon salt
1 pound cream cheese, softened
⅛ teaspoon cream of tartar
1 cup heavy cream

**TOPPING**
1 ounce semisweet baking chocolate, to make 6 chocolate curls, each 2 inches long
¼ teaspoon ground cinnamon

**PAN**
9-inch springform pan

**CRUST** In a medium-size bowl, combine the chocolate wafer crumbs, sugar, and butter. Blend well with fingers, fork, or pastry blender. Press or pat the mixture onto the bottom and sides of a well-buttered springform pan. Bake in a preheated 350°F oven for 8 minutes. Transfer to a wire rack and allow to cool completely.

FILLING   In a double boiler, blend the gelatin with the coffee liqueur and water until soft and smooth. Beat in the egg yolks, sugar, and the instant espresso dissolved in water. Add the cinnamon and half the salt, and cook the mixture, stirring, for 5 to 7 minutes, or until it thickens. Remove the pan from the heat and allow to cool slightly. In a large bowl, beat the cream cheese until smooth and creamy, then add the gelatin mixture and beat until smooth. Chill for approximately 30 minutes, or until the mixture thickens slightly. In a small mixing bowl, beat the egg whites with the cream of tartar and the remaining ⅛ teaspoon salt until the whites hold stiff peaks. In a separate bowl, beat the heavy cream until it holds stiff peaks. Fold both the egg whites and the whipped cream into the cheese mixture. Pour into the cooled pan and chill in the refrigerator, loosely covered with wax paper, for at least 3 hours, or until firm. Carefully remove the sides of the springform pan and transfer the cake to a serving dish.

TOPPING   Prepare chocolate curls by melting the chocolate, then spreading it thinly on a sheet of wax paper. Refrigerate for 30 minutes. Then, with a flat knife, scrape the chilled chocolate into curls and cut them into 2-inch long pieces. Decorate the top of the cake with the chocolate curls, sprinkle with the cinnamon, and serve.

# Cheesecakes
# with
# Fruit

## BANANA–WALNUT
## CHEESECAKE

*For this cake, the graham cracker crust extends up the sides,
the cream cheese filling is flavored with banana puree
and chopped walnuts, and the topping is sliced bananas and
finely ground walnuts. You'll savor the subtle aroma and
grainy texture of this delightful combination.*

CRUST    2 cups graham cracker crumbs
1/4 cup granulated sugar

6 tablespoons ( 3/4 stick) sweet butter, softened

FILLING    3 tablespoons unflavored gelatin
1/2 cup cold water
3 eggs, separated
1/2 cup granulated sugar
1/2 cup light cream

1 1/2 pounds cream cheese, softened
1 teaspoon vanilla extract
1 cup banana puree
1 cup chopped walnuts

TOPPING    1 cup sliced bananas

1/2 cup finely ground walnuts

PAN    10-inch springform pan

CRUST    In a medium-size bowl, combine the graham cracker crumbs, sugar, and butter. Blend well with fingers, fork, or pastry blender. Press or pat the mixture onto the bottom and sides of a well-buttered springform pan. Chill in the freezer or refrigerator for about 30 minutes.

FILLING Soften the gelatin in the cold water. In a saucepan, combine the egg yolks and sugar and gradually stir in the light cream. Cook the mixture over medium heat, stirring until it coats a metal spoon. Remove from the heat and stir in the softened gelatin. In a large bowl, beat the cream cheese until smooth, then add the vanilla and banana puree and beat until very smooth. Add the gelatin mixture to the cheese mixture and continue to beat until smooth. Fold in the chopped walnuts, then pour the mixture into the chilled springform pan and refrigerate for 3 hours.

TOPPING Carefully remove the sides of the springform pan and decorate the top of the cake with the sliced bananas. Sprinkle with the ground walnuts. Transfer the cake to a serving dish and either serve immediately or refrigerate.

# LEMON CHEESECAKE

*Truly a light, refreshing dessert. The lemon-cookie crust is covered by a layer of lemon pudding and then a soft cream cheese filling flavored with lemon rind. More interesting than plain lemon sherbet!*

**CRUST**
2 cups lemon cookie crumbs
¼ cup granulated sugar
6 tablespoons (¾ stick) sweet butter, softened

**FILLING**
1 cup cooked lemon pudding mix, warm
2 tablespoons unflavored gelatin
½ cup cold water
3 eggs, separated
¾ cup granulated sugar
½ cup light cream
1 pound cream cheese, softened
1 teaspoon lemon juice
1 tablespoon grated lemon rind
1 cup heavy cream

**PAN**
9-inch springform pan

**CRUST** In a medium-size bowl, combine the lemon cookie crumbs, sugar, and butter. Blend well with fingers, fork, or pastry blender. Press or pat the mixture onto the bottom and sides of a well-buttered springform pan. Chill in the freezer or refrigerator for 30 minutes.

**FILLING** Pour the warm lemon pudding into the chilled springform pan and refrigerate for 2 hours, or until the lemon pudding is firm. Meanwhile soften the gelatin in the cold water. In a small saucepan, combine the egg yolks and sugar and gradually stir in the light cream. Cook the mixture over medium heat, stirring, until it coats a metal spoon. Remove from the heat and stir in the softened gelatin. In a large bowl, beat the cream cheese until smooth. Add the lemon juice and grated lemon rind and beat until smooth. Add the gelatin mixture to the cheese mixture and continue to beat until smooth. Refrigerate for 30 minutes or until the mixture is set. In separate small mixing bowls, whip the heavy cream and beat the egg whites until stiff, then fold both into the chilled cheese mixture. Pour into the springform pan on top of the chilled lemon pudding. Place the cake in the refrigerator for 3 hours, or until firm. Carefully remove the sides of the springform pan, transfer the cake to a serving dish, and serve.

# ORANGE–PECAN
# CHEESECAKE

*A vanilla wafer crust flavored with orange rind. A textured cottage cheese filling flavored with orange juice and rind, and to which finely chopped pecans have been added. Decorate with mandarin orange slices for a light, warm-weather dessert.*

**CRUST**
1 cup vanilla wafer crumbs
¼ cup grated orange rind
1 tablespoon granulated sugar
3 tablespoons sweet butter, softened

**FILLING**
2 tablespoons unflavored gelatin
½ cup cold water
3 eggs, separated
¾ cup granulated sugar
⅓ cup light cream
1 pound creamed cottage cheese
2 tablespoons orange juice
1 teaspoon orange extract
1 cup heavy cream
rind of 1 orange, grated
1 cup finely chopped pecans

**TOPPING**
1 cup canned mandarin orange slices, drained

**PAN**
9-inch springform pan

**CRUST**  In a small mixing bowl, combine the vanilla wafer crumbs, grated orange rind, sugar, and butter. Blend well with fingers, fork, or pastry blender. Press or pat the mixture onto the bottom of a well-buttered springform pan. Chill in the freezer or refrigerator for 30 minutes.

**FILLING**  Soften the gelatin in the cold water. In a small saucepan, combine the egg yolks and sugar and gradually stir in the light cream. Cook the mixture over medium heat, stirring, until it coats a metal spoon. Remove from the heat and stir in the gelatin. In large bowl, beat the cottage cheese, orange juice, and orange extract until smooth. Add the gelatin mixture to the cheese mixture and beat until smooth. Chill in the refrigerator for 30 minutes or until the mixture is set. In separate small mixing bowls, whip the heavy cream and beat the egg whites until stiff, then fold both into the cheese mixture. Stir the grated orange rind and chopped pecans into the cheese mixture. Pour into the chilled pan and refrigerate for 3 hours, or until firm.

TOPPING   Carefully remove the sides of the springform pan and decorate the top of the cake with the mandarin orange slices. Transfer the cake to a serving dish and serve.

# OLD-FASHIONED PINEAPPLE CHEESECAKE

*A graham cracker crust, with a light cottage cheese filling flavored with crushed pineapple and chopped maraschino cherries, and a topping of sliced pineapple. Serve this one straight from the refrigerator for another summertime favorite.*

**CRUST**
2 cups graham cracker crumbs
¼ cup granulated sugar

6 tablespoons (¾ stick) sweet butter, softened

**FILLING**
2 cups canned crushed pineapple, drained
2 tablespoons unflavored gelatin
3 eggs, separated
¾ cup granulated sugar
½ cup light cream

1 pound creamed cottage cheese
1 teaspoon grated lemon rind
1 tablespoon lemon juice
½ cup chopped maraschino cherries
1 cup heavy cream

**TOPPING**
1 cup canned sliced pineapple, drained

**PAN**
9-inch springform pan

**CRUST** In a medium-size bowl, combine the graham cracker crumbs, sugar, and butter. Blend well with fingers, fork, or pastry blender. Press or pat the mixture onto the bottom and sides of a well-buttered springform pan. Chill in the freezer or refrigerator for about 30 minutes.

**FILLING** Drain the crushed pineapple well but reserve the juice. Soften the gelatin in the pineapple juice. In a small saucepan, combine the egg yolks and sugar and gradually blend in the

light cream. Cook the mixture over medium heat, stirring, until it coats a metal spoon. Remove from the heat and stir in the softened gelatin. In a large bowl, beat the cottage cheese until smooth and creamy. Add the grated lemon rind and lemon juice to the cottage cheese and fold the egg mixture into it. Chill for 30 minutes or until the mixture is set, then fold in the crushed pineapple and the chopped cherries. In separate small mixing bowls, whip the heavy cream and beat the egg whites until stiff, then fold both into the cheese mixture. Pour into the chilled pan and refrigerate for 3 hours, or until set and firm.

TOPPING  Carefully remove the sides of the springform pan and garnish the top of the cake with the sliced pineapple. Either serve immediately or refrigerate.

# RASPBERRY MARBLE
# CHEESECAKE

*This is an appealing rosy-hued, marbled cheesecake with
graham cracker crust and a light, textured cottage cheese filling
flavored with swirls of raspberry puree. A dessert
to delight the eye.*

CRUST     2 cups graham cracker
          crumbs
          ¼ cup granulated sugar

6 tablespoons (¾ stick)
     sweet butter, softened

FILLING   2 tablespoons unflavored
          gelatin
          ½ cup cold water
          3 eggs, separated
          ¾ cup granulated sugar
          ½ cup light cream

1 pound creamed cottage
     cheese
1 teaspoon lemon juice
1 cup heavy cream
½ cup raspberry puree

PAN       9-inch springform pan

CRUST   In a medium-size bowl, combine the graham cracker
crumbs, sugar, and butter. Blend well with fingers, fork, or pastry
blender. Press or pat the mixture onto the bottom and sides of a
well-buttered springform pan. Chill in the freezer or refrigerator
for about 30 minutes.

FILLING   Soften the gelatin in the cold water. In a small saucepan, combine the egg yolks and sugar and gradually stir in the
light cream. Cook the mixture over medium heat, stirring, until it
coats a metal spoon. Remove from heat and stir in the softened
gelatin. In a large bowl, beat the cottage cheese until very
smooth, then add the lemon juice and the gelatin mixture and
beat until smooth. Chill in the refrigerator for 30 minutes or until
the mixture is set. In separate small mixing bowls, whip the

heavy cream and beat the egg whites until stiff, then fold both into the chilled cheese mixture. Pour into the chilled springform pan. Then pour the raspberry puree into the center of the pan and, with a knife, swirl it through the cheese mixture. Refrigerate for 3 hours or until set. Carefully remove the sides of the springform pan, transfer the cake to a serving dish, and serve.

# Cheesecakes
# with
# Nuts

## TOASTED ALMOND
## CHEESECAKE

*A crunchy vanilla wafer crust containing finely chopped almonds, and a textured cottage cheese filling flavored with chopped, toasted almonds and a hint of almond extract. Delightfully cool and crunchy and a grand alternative to the usual ice cream dessert.*

**CRUST**
1 cup vanilla wafer crumbs
¼ cup finely ground almonds, toasted
¼ cup granulated sugar
3 tablespoons sweet butter, softened

**FILLING**
3 tablespoons unflavored gelatin
½ cup water
2 eggs, separated
¾ cup granulated sugar
½ cup milk
1½ pounds creamed cottage cheese
1 teaspoon almond extract
½ cup sour cream
1 cup heavy cream
1 cup finely chopped almonds, toasted

**PAN**  10-inch springform pan

**CRUST**  In a small mixing bowl, combine the vanilla wafer crumbs, ground almonds, sugar, and butter. Blend well with fingers, fork, or pastry blender. Press or pat the mixture onto the bottom of a well-buttered springform pan. Chill in the freezer or refrigerator for about 30 minutes.

FILLING   Soften the gelatin in the water. In a small saucepan, combine the egg yolks and sugar and gradually stir in the milk. Cook the mixture over medium heat, stirring, until it coats a metal spoon. Remove from the heat and stir in the gelatin. In a large bowl, beat the cottage cheese until very smooth, then add the almond extract and sour cream and beat until smooth. Add the gelatin mixture to the cheese mixture and beat again until very smooth. Chill in the refrigerator for 30 minutes or until the mixture is set. In separate small bowls, whip the heavy cream and beat the egg whites until stiff, then fold both into the cheese mixture. Stir in the chopped almonds and pour the mixture into the chilled springform pan. Refrigerate for 3 hours, or until the cake is set and firm. Carefully remove the sides of the springform pan, transfer the cake to a serving dish, and serve.

# TOASTED COCONUT CHEESECAKE

*A cool and refreshing cheesecake to serve in warm weather, this recipe features a light vanilla wafer crust, a cream cheese filling flavored with coconut milk plus shredded coconut, and a topping of delicately toasted, shredded coconut. Serve directly from the refrigerator.*

| | | |
|---|---|---|
| **CRUST** | 2 cups vanilla wafer crumbs<br>¼ cup granulated sugar | 6 tablespoons (¾ stick) sweet butter, softened |
| **FILLING** | 2 tablespoons unflavored gelatin<br>½ cup cold water<br>3 eggs, separated<br>½ cup granulated sugar<br>½ cup sweetened coconut milk | 1 pound cream cheese, softened<br>1 teaspoon vanilla extract<br>1 cup heavy cream<br>½ cup shredded coconut<br>½ cup shredded coconut, toasted |
| **PAN** | 9-inch springform pan | |

**CRUST** In a medium-size bowl, combine the vanilla wafer crumbs, sugar, and butter. Blend well with fingers, fork, or pastry blender. Press or pat the mixture onto the bottom and sides of a well-buttered springform pan. Chill in the freezer or refrigerator for 30 minutes.

**FILLING** Soften the gelatin in the cold water. In a small saucepan, combine the egg yolks and sugar and gradually stir in the coconut milk. Cook the mixture over medium heat, stirring, until it coats a metal spoon. Remove from the heat and stir in the softened gelatin. In a large bowl, beat the cream cheese until very smooth and creamy, then add the vanilla and continue to beat until smooth. Add the gelatin mixture to the cheese mixture and beat until smooth. Chill in the refrigerator for 30 minutes or until the mixture is set. In separate small mixing bowls, whip the heavy cream and beat the egg whites until stiff. Fold both the whipped cream and the egg whites into the cheese mixture. Mix in the shredded coconut, then pour the mixture into the chilled springform pan. Sprinkle the toasted coconut over the top of the cake and refrigerate for 3 hours. Carefully remove the sides of the springform pan, transfer the cake to a serving dish, and serve.

---

# HAZELNUT CHEESECAKE

*The ultimate in cheese-nut combinations, this cake's graham cracker crust contains finely ground hazelnuts and the extra creamy filling is diffused with chopped hazelnuts. Elegant is the operable word—no topping could enhance this subtle creation.*

**CRUST**

1¾ cups graham cracker crumbs
½ cup finely ground hazelnuts

¼ cup granulated sugar
6 tablespoons ( ¾ stick) sweet butter, softened

**FILLING**

2 tablespoons unflavored gelatin
½ cup cold water
3 eggs, separated
¾ cup granulated sugar
½ cup light cream

1 pound cream cheese, softened
1 teaspoon vanilla extract
1 teaspoon lemon juice
1 cup heavy cream
1 cup finely chopped hazelnuts

**PAN**

9-inch springform pan

CRUST  In a medium-size bowl, combine the graham cracker crumbs, ground hazelnuts, sugar, and butter. Blend well with fingers, fork, or pastry blender. Press or pat the mixture onto the bottom and sides of a well-buttered springform pan. Chill in the freezer or refrigerator for 30 minutes.

FILLING  Soften the gelatin in the cold water. In a small saucepan, combine the egg yolks and sugar and gradually stir in the light cream. Cook the mixture over medium heat, stirring, until it coats a metal spoon. Remove from the heat and stir in the softened gelatin. In a large bowl, beat the cream cheese until very smooth and creamy, then add the vanilla and lemon juice and beat until smooth. Add the gelatin mixture to the cheese mixture and beat until smooth. Chill in the refrigerator for 30 minutes or until the mixture is set. In separate small mixing bowls, whip the heavy cream and beat the egg whites until stiff, then fold both into the chilled cheese mixture. Stir the chopped hazelnuts evenly into the mixture. Pour into the chilled springform pan and refrigerate for 3 hours, or until set. Carefully remove the sides of the springform pan, transfer the cake to a serving dish, and serve.

# MIXED NUTS AND RAISINS CHEESECAKE

*The complementary tastes and textures of nuts and raisins—
who can resist them? This recipe combines both with
cream cheese and a graham cracker crust for a
naturally appealing dessert.*

**CRUST**

1 cup graham cracker crumbs
2 tablespoons granulated sugar
3 tablespoons sweet butter, softened

**FILLING**

2 tablespoons unflavored gelatin
½ cup cold water
3 eggs, separated
¾ cup granulated sugar
½ cup light cream
1 pound cream cheese, softened
1 teaspoon lemon juice
1 teaspoon vanilla extract
1 cup heavy cream
1 cup mixed chopped nuts (hazelnuts, pecans, walnuts)
¾ cup seedless raisins

**PAN**  9-inch springform pan

**CRUST**  In a small mixing bowl, combine the graham cracker crumbs, sugar, and butter. Blend well with fingers, fork, or pastry blender. Press or pat the mixture onto the bottom of a well-buttered springform pan. Chill in the freezer or the refrigerator for about 30 minutes.

**FILLING**  Soften the gelatin in the cold water. In a small saucepan, combine the egg yolks and sugar and stir in the light cream. Cook the mixture over medium heat, stirring, until it coats a metal spoon. Remove from the heat and stir in the softened gelatin. In large bowl, beat the cream cheese, lemon juice, and vanilla until smooth. Add the gelatin mixture to the cheese mixture and beat until smooth. Chill in the refrigerator for 30 minutes or until the mixture is set. In separate small mixing bowls, whip the heavy cream and beat the egg whites until stiff, then fold both into the chilled cheese mixture. Stir in the mixed nuts and raisins. Pour the mixture into the chilled springform pan and refrigerate for 3 hours, or until firm. Carefully remove the sides of the springform pan, transfer the cake to a serving dish, and serve.

———————

# Cheesecakes from Around the World

## AMERICAN BUTTERSCOTCH CHEESECAKE

*Here's a unique cake—a butter cookie crust, a creamy filling flavored with lemon juice, rum extract, and butterscotch pudding, and a topping of finely ground hazelnuts. Served cold for an appetizing cheesecake variation.*

**CRUST**
1 cup butter cookie crumbs
1 tablespoon granulated sugar
2 tablespoons sweet butter, softened

**FILLING**
2 tablespoons unflavored gelatin
½ cup cold water
3 eggs, separated
½ cup granulated sugar
⅓ cup light cream
1 pound cream cheese, softened
1 teaspoon lemon juice
1 teaspoon rum extract
1 cup heavy cream
2 cups cooked butterscotch pudding mix, lukewarm

**TOPPING**
½ cup finely ground hazelnuts

**PAN**
10-inch springform pan

CRUST  In a small mixing bowl, combine the butter cookie crumbs, sugar, and butter. Blend well with fingers, fork, or pastry blender. Press or pat the mixture onto the bottom of a well-buttered springform pan. Chill in the freezer or the refrigerator for about 30 minutes.

FILLING  Soften the gelatin in the cold water. In a small saucepan, combine the egg yolks and sugar and gradually stir in the light cream. Cook the mixture over medium heat, stirring, until it coats a metal spoon. Remove from the heat and stir in the softened gelatin. In large bowl, beat the cream cheese, lemon juice, and rum extract until smooth. Add the gelatin mixture to the cheese mixture and beat until very smooth. Chill in the refrigerator for 30 minutes or until the mixture is set. In separate small mixing bowls, whip the heavy cream and beat the egg whites until stiff, then fold both into the cheese mixture. Add the lukewarm butterscotch pudding and mix well.

TOPPING  Pour the mixture into the chilled springform pan and sprinkle the ground hazelnuts on top. Refrigerate for 3 hours, or until firm. Carefully remove the sides of the springform pan, transfer the cake to a serving dish, and serve.

# ALASKAN CHEESECAKE

*A cheesecake with the texture of ice cream but far less sugar!
This can be prapared in advance and kept in the freezer
till time to thaw and serve. A crust of vanilla wafers
and shredded coconut, a creamy cream cheese filling flavored
with crushed strawberries, and a topping of whipped cream
sprinkled with chopped walnuts make this a bountiful treat.*

| | | |
|---|---|---|
| **CRUST** | 1 cup vanilla wafer crumbs | ½ cup shredded coconut |
| | 2 tablespoons granulated sugar | 3 tablespoons sweet butter, softened |
| **FILLING** | 1 pound cream cheese, softened | ½ teaspoon vanilla extract |
| | 4 eggs, separated | 1 cup heavy cream |
| | 1 cup honey | 1 cup crushed fresh strawberries |
| | ⅛ teaspoon salt | |
| **TOPPING** | 1 cup heavy cream, whipped | ½ cup finely chopped walnuts |
| **PAN** | 9-inch springform pan | |

**CRUST** In a small mixing bowl, combine the vanilla wafer crumbs, sugar, coconut, and butter. Blend well with fingers, fork, or pastry blender. Press or pat the mixture onto the bottom of an ungreased springform pan and bake in a preheated 350°F oven for 8 minutes. Transfer to a wire rack and allow to cool for 20 minutes.

**FILLING** In a large bowl, beat the cream cheese and egg yolks until smooth. Add the honey, salt, and vanilla and beat until smooth and light. In a small mixing bowl, whip the heavy cream, then fold it into the cream cheese mixture. In separate bowl, beat the egg whites until they form a stiff peak, then fold them into the cheese mixture. Pour into the springform pan. With a spoon, drop the strawberries into the center of the mixture, then swirl them through. Place the cake in the freezer for 3½ hours or longer.

TOPPING  Remove the cake from the freezer about 1½ hours before serving and decorate the top with the whipped cream and chopped walnuts. Let stand at room temperature for at least another 30 minutes before serving.

# SPANISH RUM CHEESECAKE

*Rich aroma and taste to please the cheesecake aficionado.
This recipe combines a crust of graham crackers and finely
ground pistachios, a soft cream cheese filling flavored with dark
Spanish rum, and a topping of rum-flavored sour cream
dotted with bits of orange rind.*

**CRUST**
1 cup graham cracker
  crumbs
½ cup finely ground
  pistachio nuts

¼ cup granulated sugar
3 tablespoons sweet
  butter, softened

**FILLING**
1 tablespoon unflavored
  gelatin
¾ cup dark rum
¼ cup lime juice
4 eggs, separated
1 pound cream cheese,
  softened

⅛ teaspoon cream of
  tartar
⅛ teaspoon salt
½ cup granulated sugar
1 cup heavy cream

**TOPPING**
1½ cups sour cream
1 teaspoon rum extract

¼ cup granulated sugar
¼ cup grated orange rind

**PAN**
9-inch springform pan

**CRUST**  In a medium-size bowl, combine the graham cracker
crumbs, ground pistachio nuts, sugar, and butter. Blend well with
fingers, fork, or pastry blender. Press or pat the mixture onto the
bottom and sides of a well-buttered springform pan. Chill in the
freezer or refrigerator for 30 minutes.

**FILLING**  In the top of a double boiler, blend the gelatin with the
rum and lime juice until smooth and soft. Set the pan over boiling
water and bring the liquid to a simmer, stirring. Beat in the egg
yolks, one at a time, and cook the mixture, stirring, until it begins

to thicken. Remove from the heat and allow to cool slightly. In a large bowl, beat the cream cheese and sugar together until smooth and creamy. Add the gelatin mixture, beat until smooth, and refrigerate for 30 minutes. In a small mixing bowl, beat the egg whites with the cream of tartar and salt until the whites hold stiff peaks. In a separate bowl, beat the heavy cream until it holds stiff peaks. Fold both the egg whites and the whipped cream into the cheese mixture. Pour into the chilled pan and refrigerate, loosely covered with wax paper, for at least 3 hours, or until firm.

TOPPING In a medium-size bowl, beat the sour cream, rum extract, and sugar until smooth. Spread the mixture evenly over the top of the cake and sprinkle with grated orange rind. Chill for 2 hours. Carefully remove the sides of the springform pan, transfer the cake to a serving dish, and serve. For best results, remove the cake from the refrigerator at least 2 hours before serving.

# INDEX

# Index